The ADHD and Abuse-Damaged Brain

A Guide for Survivors and Their Companions

Brent A. Vogt, Ph.D.

The ADHD and Abuse-Damaged Brain
A Guide for Survivors and Their Companions
All Rights Reserved.
Copyright © 2020 Cingulum Neurosciences Institute
v5.0

The opinions expressed in this manuscript are solely the opinions of the author and do not represent the opinions or thoughts of the publisher. The author has represented and warranted full ownership and/or legal right to publish all the materials in this book.

This book may not be reproduced, transmitted, or stored in whole or in part by any means, including graphic, electronic, or mechanical without the express written consent of the publisher except in the case of brief quotations embodied in critical articles and reviews.

Outskirts Press, Inc.
http://www.outskirtspress.com

ISBN: 978-0-578-23452-6

Cover & interior images by Brent A. Vogt © 2020. All rights reserved - used with permission.

Cingulum Neurosciences Institute

PRINTED IN THE UNITED STATES OF AMERICA

The cover is a modified self portrait of the author when he was 21 years old showing the turmoil of his mental state as an Attention-Deficit/Hyperactivity Disorder (ADHD) and abuse survivor. His Christian Fundamentalist parents did not understand his behaviors as mediated by ADHD and tried to beat them out of him to no effect. The inscription "Dead Birds Fly" refers to his depressive views during this transition period that one cannot trust what they see as a true reflection of reality. A fire burns in his chest. The oval over his left ear shows brain cells (neurons) that store information in the brain and are damaged in survivors. The top photograph is of the middle part of the brain showing damage to cingulate cortex from multiple studies of ADHD and abuse survivors. This series of images emphasizes that while a survivor's face and behaviors are the visible results of ADHD and abuse, the problems they suffer are located throughout the body and in the brain by groups of neurons. His maltreatment led to anxiety, bipolar, borderline personality and posttraumatic stress disorders. ADHD and abuse evoke serious brain injuries that are still not understood or well treated.

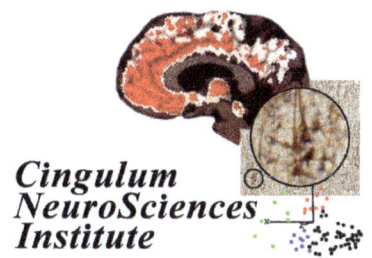

Cingulum NeuroSciences Institute

Dedications

IT IS A great joy that I dedicate this book to my wife. She has seen me through the ups and downs of a life metamorphosis that most women would have been unable to face. She played a major role in my coming to resolution of the many psychiatric difficulties that arose from genes and an abusive adolescence that even I did not understand when we were married more than 30 years ago. She has worked with me in the laboratory to understand cingulate cortex structure, functions and adolescent abuse and her histology formed the basis on which a long and productive career was built. Her strength is obvious and our relationship is a love story that made this work possible.

I also appreciate the input from my sister Betsy and daughter Emily as I watched them both struggle with different issues throughout their lives. They both contributed in different ways to my personal insights in this book.

I would be remiss if I did not dedicate this book to the millions of individuals with ADHD and abuse survivors around the world. This book was written for them and the people they know and try to understand their behavior and provide treatments. The child and adolescent experiences we confront are difficult to understand from outside of the brain and are imprinted by genetic and environmental forces that shape our personalities including a wide range of emotional responses.

Acknowledgments. I thank my lifetime colleague Dr. Ellen Townes-Anderson for making important suggestions for revisions of this book. Also, Mr. Ken Rovtar, a Safety Officer at the NYS Office of People with Developmental Disabilities, made important textual suggestions.

Preface

MY BRAIN WAS first genetically damaged by Attention-Deficit/Hyperactivity Disorder (ADHD) with behavioral (cognitive and social) and educational delay recognized at around the age of 7. The behaviors evoked various forms of abuse due to the aggression and strict fundamentalist beliefs of my parents and this evolved into posttraumatic stress syndrome (PTSD), Borderline Personality, anxiety and Bipolar Disorders. As I chose to study neuroscience rather than ride some of the more ominous outcomes of adolescent abuse (substance abuse, violence leading to jail time, abusing adolescents, suicide, etc.), this story intertwines a life with these disorders and neuroscience. I know of no other book that interprets the personal, psychiatric account of a survivor's life with that of a neuroscience perspective. This story is instructive as it follows cause and effect over 60+ years to see how ADHD and abuse evokes a cascade of events that engender further issues and difficulties layered onto them. A number of psychotherapeutic and drug treatments had value in my adulthood and should be considered by survivors of all ages. No reader's life will follow the same steps as mine, but there will be many similarities and shared experiences. This book will take survivors and their companions and caregivers into the confused brain produced by ADHD and abuse and may help in seeing through their problems and assist in the survivor's efforts to build a family and succeed professionally in spite of their adolescent traumatic upbringing.

Table of Contents

Dedications i
Preface iii
Vignette 1:   An Investigational Psychoautobiography
                & General Issues: 1
Vignette 2:   A Short Lesson in Cingulate Neuropathology 13
Vignette 3:   Attention-Deficit/Hyperactivity Disorder 20
Vignette 4:   What is Abuse, Frequency and Consequences? 41
Vignette 5:   Parental Histories 47
Vignette 6:   "Jesus Saves" 50
Vignette 7:   Blanche E. Smith (Vogt): A Parental Predator 52
Vignette 8:   The First Beating: My ADHD Made Me Do It! 61
Vignette 9:   The Coronet: An Evangelical Instrument
                and Severe Stress. 65
Vignette 10: Stanley: The Obedient Soldier and Further Beatings . . 69
Vignette 11: Child Abuse Reporting & Penalties. 72
Vignette 12: Strong Links Between Maltreatment and PTSD. 76
Vignette 13: Refuge in the Basement. 82

Vignette 14: The Vogt Family as a Model of
            Poor Social Bonding 87
Vignette 15: Sex 90
Vignette 16: Art Expresses Emotion and Internal Turmoil 94
Vignette 17: *Jesus Christ Superstar* 102
Vignette 18: Transition to Adulthood: Building a New Person . . . 104
Vignette 19: Marriage #1 108
Vignette 20: Adventure in the Northwest Territories 112
Vignette 21: Psychotherapy: Marco, BPD and DBT 116
Vignette 22: Empathy 122
Vignette 23: Neuro-Psycho-Pharmacology 126
Vignette 24: The Dawn of Modern Neuroscience
            and a Key Discovery 131
Vignette 25: Founding of Cingulum Neurosciences Institute 137
Vignette 26: First Mental Breakdown 140
Vignette 27: Second Mental Breakdown 144
Vignette 28: From Intension Tremors to Near Death 147
Vignette 29: Classical Conditioning, the
            Placebo Effect and Abuse 152
Vignette 30: "True" Belief & Free Will versus
            Genes & Environment 155
Vignette 31: What is Suffering? 163
Vignette 32: The Cycle of Violence 167
Vignette 33: Can Animal Research Help Understand
            & Cure Abuse Survivors? 174
Overall Conclusions 184

VIGNETTE 1

An Investigational Psychoautobiography & General Issues

THIS BOOK IS an *investigational psychoautobiography*. It is not just a reflection on the psychiatric phenomena of my life as appear in many autobiographies or memoirs. In both of the latter instances, authors consider the details of their life in a story format without trying to uncover the neurological meaning of their history, how events are linked and evolve into other disorders, influence their adult life, and how they might help others generalize and cope with similar experiences. This volume is an effort to interpret my behaviors from inside the brain but not too much, I hope, so that the reader will become bewildered with details. It is also an effort to intertwine my long history of psychiatric issues and neuroscientific views into a cohesive story line. I found this process itself to be therapeutic as writing or "journaling" can be a useful form of artistic expression. For me it helped to make sense of what appears at first to be a bewildering set of events.

Thus, rather than stopping at the reported phenomena in my life, as a neuroscientist, I am interested in *cause and effect*. In other words, one or more events can evoke a cascade of changes in the brain throughout one's life; i.e., Attention-Deficit/Hyperactivity Disorder

The ADHD and Abuse-Damaged Brain

(ADHD) and abuse are not isolated events that simply go away in the brain but rather have many long-term and negative consequences including evoking posttraumatic stress disorder (PTSD), anxiety and Bipolar and Borderline Personality Disorders.

One's life struggles can enlighten others and help them come to terms with their own experiences and my life is one such example. As I turn the musty and yellowing pages of my memory, there are still many clear images of times, places and people that led to my adult understanding of my life as an adolescent with ADHD and as an abuse survivor. Some of the memories were stored in my brain with high Fidelity on a substrate of emotional arousal; for example, when you fear something, you are more likely to remember it than when you do not. Memories that are not tagged with an emotional signature like severe fear, pain and stress are often lost in the complex networks of our brains. Also, the passage of time relieves us of some of the negative memories and active dissociation from some experiences can block less intense episodes. In some ways my experiences are not much different from those of other adolescents with ADHD, abused, neglected and emotionally maltreated histories. My insights and suggestions from more than 60 years may be helpful to those who suffer with such histories and possibly proactively prevent them from visiting various forms of abuse on others including their families in what is later referred to as the Cycle of Violence.

Let us consider a few artists whose stories are well known.

Antwone Fisher, director, screenwriter, author, and film producer presented his 2001 autobiographical book *"Finding Fishin"* and in 2002 the American biographical drama film directed by one of my favorite actor/directors Denzel Washington. It tells a story of maternal neglect, a father killed before he was born, and the struggles and torment by his step mother. Besides the book and movie, a senate hearing titled "The Antwone Fisher Story as a Case Study for Child Welfare" documents his testimony (see finance.senate.gov/imo/media/doc/86847.pdf). "I endured, along with my foster siblings, sexual abuse, verbal abuse, physical - anything you can imagine, they rained this down on us. And I endured this with my foster siblings for 12 years." As an adult he was withdrawn, had no meaningful female relationships, was extremely angry and quick to engage in conflict and fighting. In spite of all this, he was able to build a productive career.

Alan Cumming, the Broadway actor and film producer, wrote a book titled "Not My Father's Son" (2015; First Dey Street Books) that recounts his violent experiences at the hands of an abusive father and how it impacted his adolescence and reverberated throughout his adult life. I read the book to see how his maltreatment affected his adulthood and the following sentences stood out. "I wondered, if I didn't have the job I have, which provides me with such thrilling, visceral release, would I be seeking those thrills in destructive ways? I know I love the rush of adrenaline pulsing through my veins. I wonder to what lengths I would go to experience it if I didn't do what I do?" Thus, like many artists, Alan Cumming finds solace in his artistic career and relationships.

Beth Hart. When listening one evening to "War in My Mind," I knew immediately that this woman has an internal struggle to express through her art. Her lyric video of this song emphasizes the brain. Of this piece she said, "… on this album, I'm even closer to vulnerability and openness about my life, about love, addiction, my bipolar, my dad, my sister…" An interview with her by Don Wilcock in 2016 for *Blues Blast* had a number of interesting quotes. She said, "Her childhood was scarred by a rocky relationship with her father. When I was a kid, my dad left me in a bad way, and what f***ed me up the most was that he would be in the lives of my other sisters and brothers, but he wouldn't be in mine." She also struggled with substance abuse and songs like *"Trouble"* and *"St. Theresa"* on *"Better Than Home"* boil with anger and angst. She said, "What I care about is being able to connect to it on a level that I call a family level, a root level where you start out in life. And if I can connect it to that place, then I know I'm the right person to be singing it at that time." Producer Michael Stevens told her, "Forget the blues. Forget the rock chick. Forget the screaming and hollering. Just tell me a story. *Tell me how you really feel.*" The interview is completed with her saying, "I've come a long way with healing, and I'm comfortable with my darknesses, weirdnesses and things that I'm ashamed of – as well as all the things that make me feel good."

The goal of this book is to help each reader (survivor, parent, companion or friend) get into their own head and the heads of their family members and friends that may suffer from one or more of the disorders discussed herein. This is not an easy task as our society controls against entering another person's mental space; their cone of personal space if you will. Mores about what is appropriate for discussion usually block such an effort and the many life events associated with shame, embarrassment, fear and judgmental views of the person suffering. Healthy observers attempt to overlook these events as untouchable; a childhood incestuous rape, a priest's rape of altar boys; athletic coaches raping their sportsman (Jerry Sandusky at Penn State is an example), physical abuse by a parent or family "friend" and often foster parents as those encountered by Antwone Fisher. Unfortunately, if these issues and their consequences cannot be openly discussed, they cannot be addressed and fixed. Survivors with ADHD and child and adolescent abuse cannot be expected to live with the brain damage evoked by their genes and abuse, much less not discuss it. Many, if not most, turn to powerful drugs including opioids like oxycodone or cocaine to self-medicate their pain and suffering. Later in this book, we will consider the late Dr. Marco Alfondary, the psychotherapist who helped me open the hood of my cranium non-judgmentally and look at the psychiatric puss that I was carrying in my brain so that we could lance it and I could move on to the next stage of my life rather than being locked into a life of overwhelming suffering and drug abuse.

Book format. This volume is presented as a series of vignettes (little stories) with titles because of their different lengths and content that enhances seeing relationships among different parts of my ADHD and various forms of abuse and other psychiatric issues that emerged therefrom including PTSD. Some vignettes are only a few pages long; hardly what one might term a chapter *per se*. In addition to vignettes, there are a few fanciful, tongue-in-cheek stories from fictitious newspapers and sarcastic comments sprinkled along the way to add a bit of humor to the generally dour subject matter. The artwork is my own as it tells my story in a different, more powerful and emotional way.

Many vignettes begin with my personal experience(s) and at the end there is a summary, conclusions and/or suggestions for survivors and their companions and caretakers that often work with them on these very personal issues. In many places the text moves beyond my personal experiences to consider broader issues in larger populations. These generalizations should help the reader make contact with what is said even if my issues do not exactly correlate with their own. There are some literature citations for the interested reader to pursue further reading but the text is not written as a scientific work with extensive citations to document each thought. Citations in Vignette 2 and others, for example, must be provided when referring to the findings of specific imaging studies. Some of the journals are open access and do not charge for the articles such as the *Frontiers* journals, while most require payment or access to a medical school library's electronic journals. If you trust my interpretations, these can be overlooked.

I do not feign being a psychiatrist or psychotherapist; I am not. I am simply a neuroscientist trying to understand how the brain works and dos not work under the genetic and environmental conditions of ADHD and child and adolescent abuse and other psychopathologies. As a neuroscientist, I require evidence of organic changes in the brain for various therapeutic interventions so that we are not simply following belief systems that make people feel good and can be misleading. The suggestions at the end of some vignettes are guidelines from my 60+ years of experience that the reader may consider relevant to their life and those of others that have experienced ADHD and maltreatment and their companions that want to better understand their turmoil with finding a resolution in mind.

My adolescence was basically a parental and family problem (adolescence is between 7 and 18 or 25 years of age, although children between ages 3-6 are also abused), an interactive problem between my parents, myself and sister. My ADHD interfered with family relationships as it does for many such patients and Blanche's effort to keep me from my brother was problematic. Stanley's willingness to physically abuse me clearly set blocks in our relationship. I later married into a functional family and this is how I learned much about family cohesiveness and rules for relating. Other survivors of abuse and neglect may resort to aggression and some of those with severe psychopathy maim or kill and spend much of their life in prison.

While the variation in individual life experiences is high and I do not expect any one person to follow the same course of events as in my life, much less become a neuroscientist, it provides an approach that is a road map for others to explore their experiences. Indeed, there will be many similarities among experiences of ADHD and abused children and adolescents that should provide insight into their lives even if there is not an exact replication of them; hence, the notion of an *"investigational psychoautobiography"* that emphasizes my psychiatric issues, of which there are many, and how to interpret them.

As we take this journey together you will find it personal, artistic and scientific. Most of the vignettes begin with personal experiences as best I can recall them and reflections on what they meant to me and how they affected my adult life for more than 60 years. It was difficult (depressing) at many points to resurrect these memories, particularly later in the text on the Cycle of Violence vignette to see how, though trying to break this Cycle, I was unable to completely do so partly due to my lack of an understanding of what constituted abuse as I thought it was defined from the perspective of my birth family as harsh physical abuse. As it is often said, "if only I knew then what I know now."

My scientific need to identify cause and effect is followed along a lifeline. In instances there are artistic outcroppings from me that reflect on the external features of the abused adolescent. However, this is but a stepping stone to understand broader psychiatric and brain dysfunction issues; an understanding that will, in the long run, I hope, lead to permanent treatments for the survivors of abuse rather than transitory taking of illicit drugs and violence. The scientific observations that led me on this life mission are presented in lay terms so as to be accessible to those who prefer not to spend 50 years studying the structure, functions and diseases of cingulate cortex; a particularly vulnerable part of the brain to ADHD, maltreatment and PTSD. Only select findings are presented that I consider important to understand the brains of my "brothers and sisters" that survived ADHD and abuse. Together we will understand and cure their immense suffering.

Normal, healthy individuals. If you have suffered with depresssion, anxiety, PTSD symptoms, and ADHD or other psychiatric disease(s), you will readily identify with parts of this text and from there to an understanding of much else that is being said about the lives of abused children in particular and psychiatric disease in general, whether or not you have such histories. However, in my view, some readers are essentially normal and mentally healthy. While introductory psychology classes banter back and forth over whether or not there are normal and abnormal individuals, I am convinced of two things: First, I am clearly *not* normal; as you will see throughout this text, and second, my son is relatively healthy. I know this latter fact because I changed almost every one of his diapers as a toddler, put every vegetable (including broccoli) into his mouth when he was a child, cared for typical adolescent issues including a brief trip into the town legal system to the fine adult that he is today as a successful business man with a degree in sustainable energy management.

Normal, healthy individuals are people in my view with a generally quiet genome and child/adolescent environmental history. They clearly identify their work boundaries and restrict themselves to socially accepted norms. Their views and responses are those of individuals with little or no psychiatric disease possibly requiring only an occasional period of psychotherapy and live without or only minor drug interventions. I think that the presumption made by normal individuals is that everyone is essentially the same and a few tweaks will bring them into line with the rest of society. Sadly, this is not true as the brain of survivors is seriously impaired and still not amenable to being completely cured of its deficits. The non-normals, of which I am one, perceive facts, balance perspectives and logic in ways that are not the same. Inevitably, their solutions are not the same either. This all boils down to saying, if you are generally a healthy normal, your brain and behavior are very different from mine. This is one of the key purposes of this book; to explore these differences.

Finally, to be normal does not mean one's life is a matter of perfection as almost everyone assumes when I broach this concept. It means, in my opinion, that while everyone has anxieties, fears, compulsions, and some suffer from the trauma of cancer or neurological diseases, or death of loved ones during most of their adult lives, they are not distracted by such psychiatric impairments in their everyday life. When the term "normals" and "healthy" are used herein, they mean "essentially" free of debilitating psychiatric and neurological diseases. The normal individual in my understanding is one who needs less than 6 months of psychotherapy and only a short period of psychotropic drug therapy (6-12 months), if at all. It is crucial for the reader to identify whether or not they are normal and healthy in this usage because, if one is, they are looking into the head of another, in this instance of the ADHD, maltreated and/or PTSD survivor, and cannot fully appreciate what is being said from that person's introspective, emotional perspective.

One help in understanding the following text is reflecting on one's family members or friends who do so suffer. Many years of observing family interactions suggests to me that no family is completely free of at least a minimum of some genetic disability in one or more members. Even when some members try to hide such difficulties, careful observation and conversation uncovers many difficult behaviors, and conversation on these issues raises the problems that some family members suffer with. I purposefully attempt to break the barrier between myself and others and it is surprising how many individuals have experienced harsh physical abuse and rape and other forms of abuse. These conversations also underpin what you are about to read.

Are you vulnerable or resilient to maltreatment and stress? Stress research constantly reports there are some individuals that are vulnerable

An Investigational Psychoautobiography & General Issues

to pain and/or stress and others that are not; the latter being resilient. For example, you can compare the life stories of two adult women that were sexually abused as children. In the former instance of a vulnerable woman, she often reports early and adult problems with substance abuse for self-medication, a varying amount of psychotherapy and ongoing suffering. In the latter case of a resilient woman there are no such reports. The same is true for soldiers who engaged in multiple tours of duty. Some develop PTSD, and others exposed to a similar level of battle do not; vulnerable in the first instance and resilient in the latter one. While I suspect that resilient individuals in fact have some long-term defects in brain function, this will need to be resolved with objective markers of brain impairments that we do not yet have. Also, the human population is quite variable genetically and to environmental exposures and it is difficult to calibrate the level of abuse so that we are comparing apples with apples as in the two-woman example above. Nonetheless, some women report a relatively unimpaired life following their maltreatment and we refer to them as being resilient. This book is about mainly vulnerable individuals as they are the group mainly in need of treatment and that is what I am.

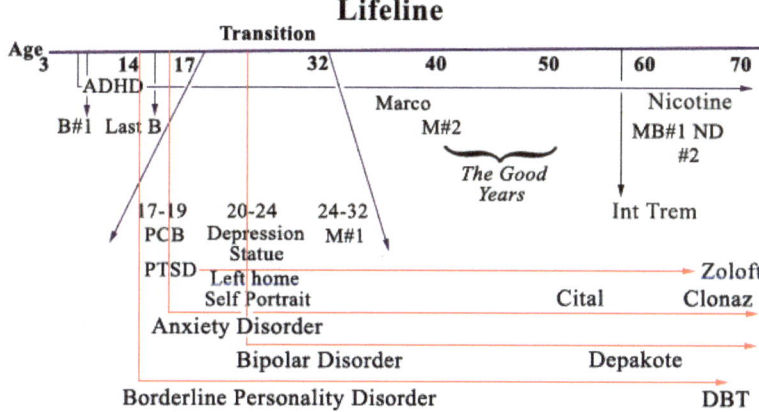

Key: B#1 & Last Beating
PTSD, posttraumatic stress disorder
M#1, Marriage #1
M#2, Marriage #2
MB#1 & #2, Mental Breakdowns
DBT, Dialectical Behavioral Therapy
PCB, Philadelphia College of Bible
Cital, Citalopram
Clonaz, Clonazepam
Int Trem, Intension tremors
ND, Near Death

My Lifeline and brief summary. My effort to identify cause and effect is based on a Lifeline as shown in this picture. The Lifeline connects the dots of my life. No events in my life are independent of the initiating factor of ADHD and from the often bizarre behaviors resulting from the disorder. I was not diagnosed at each time point with the many psychopathologies that are shown. I have drawn these conclusions about them from 1) recalled events, 2) reports of teachers, 3) later diagnoses, 4) psychotherapeutic responses, and 5) particular drug efficacies. Throughout my life I often engaged in therapeutic activities by accident rather than direction by qualified professionals except for that with the late Dr. Marco Alfondary and Dialectical Behavioral Therapy (DBT). As an overview of my life, the Lifeline shows key events and how they are linked. In other words, it is an outline of this book.

When considering your life, you might draft such a lifeline to help understand how the dots in your life are linked. If you are still in the prime of your life, say 25-45 years old, you might look at past events and future plans as part of your lifeline such as where have I been and where am I going? The early part of my Lifeline was dominated by Fundamentalist religious experience beginning with a conversion/salvation at 3-4 years of age and terminating with a short stint at the Philadelphia College of Bible (PCB). This period was also dominated by ADHD, anxiety and Borderline Personality (BPD) disorders that are highly comorbid (combined disorders rather than a single diagnosis) and lasted through my entire life until DBT with my daughter assisted us both in coping with ADHD and BPD. Notice the arrow for ADHD extending from ~7 years of age when it became apparent from teacher reports and some of my "out of the ordinary" behaviors and lasting to the present. Moreover, its appearance closely approximates when my parents started beating me. This is not surprising as you will see.

I estimate that Bipolar Disorder (BD) began in about the middle of my Transitional Period and is well treated today with Clonazepam. Success of the later treatments confirmed the conclusions about earlier times in my life such as the drug Depakote (also termed valproate) for

BD. The Transition Period was a time of stress as well as that evoked earlier by harsh physical abuse. This transition began in my early 20s as I broke the chains of strict religion that were strangling me and lasted until the end of my first marriage at age 32. The events during this time are broken into three parts as shown on the Lifeline. Psychotherapy later with the late Dr. Marco Alfondary helped me break the wall that was preventing me from moving on from this period into more healthy, adult relationships including a second marriage that began what I term "The Good Years." This is not to say that my psychiatric disturbances had been alleviated; only that they were submerged to some extent by the overwhelming joy of my second marriage and the birth of our two children in North Carolina. Here we bought a home in rural Winston-Salem, NC and enjoyed vacations in the Blue Ridge Mountains and North Carolina coastline with our young children. Friendships were easily formed and maintained at this time.

Unfortunately, my various psychopathologies had not and never will be completely resolved and I carry them in my brain to this day and this undergirds my professional activities. An insightful physician realized that I was suffering with an anxiety disorder and prescribed citalopram that was helpful in remediating this problem. Indeed, it even helped me with my ADHD and BPD to some extent including aggressive driving habits. I remember driving down a street in Upstate New York one day thinking, "Is this what it is like to be normal; unpressured to drive fast, tailgate and pass the car ahead of me?" This drug was later switched to Clonazapam which appears to be more effective in relieving my adult anxiety. Later it became clear that my depression and mania (BD) also had not resolved and I was placed on Depakote/valproate that was helpful but caused problems at a high dose by inducing intention tremors (i.e., when doing precise work, mainly with my right hand, it would shake) and even later an additional drug evoked near death experiences. When reduced to half dose, Depakote alone is still effective for BD and does not evoke intention tremors. My demons had not been vanquished, however, and I had two mental breakdowns that are periods of intense mental stress when one's emotion mind takes complete control and overt behaviors become irrational and are virtually impossible to deal with.

Many disorders in a long life. As I have expressed many disorders throughout my life, it is necessary to consider their evolution and treatments that are helpful to me as an adult. The following picture shows these in a categorical summary in contrast to the temporal summary of my Lifeline. It contains each disorder, as I think they evolved from each other (black arrows) and the vignette number in parentheses where they are discussed in some detail. This diagram should help the reader to stay organized while following the text of a very complicated life; particularly with issues and relationships that may not be readily apparent at first. It should be noted that if one has a single, isolated disorder, this more complex evolution may not be relevant to one's mental health. With that said as an overview, let us begin exploring a life impaired by numerous psychopathologies

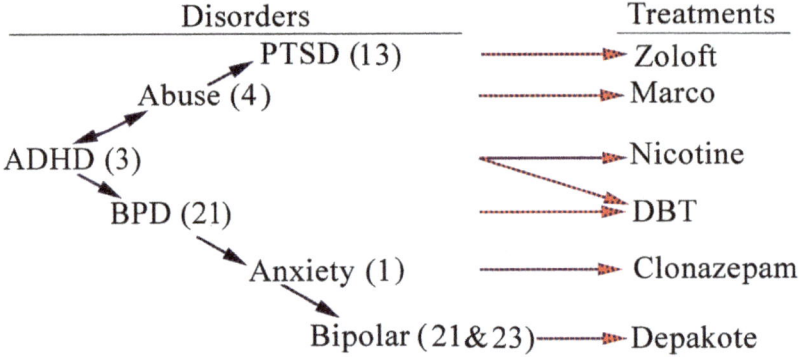

Key: ADHD, Attention-Deficit/Hperactivity Disorder
    BPD, Borderline Personality Disorder
    PTSD, Posttraumatic Stress Disorder
    Bipolar, Bipolar Disorder
    DBT, Dialectical Behavioral Therapy
    Vignette numbers in parentheses

VIGNETTE 2

A Short Lesson in Cingulate Neuropathology

THERE ARE NOW dozens of brain imaging studies that evaluate the brain structure and functions of ADHD and various forms of abuse. In spite of this intense interest, there are still substantial variations in conclusions due to differences in patient populations (age, sex, socioeconomic background, etc.) and methods of data analysis. Here we focus on cingulate cortex which is one of the most frequently damaged regions in the disorders under consideration but non-cingulate areas are also involved in each including other regions that form the limbic system and are engaged in emotion.

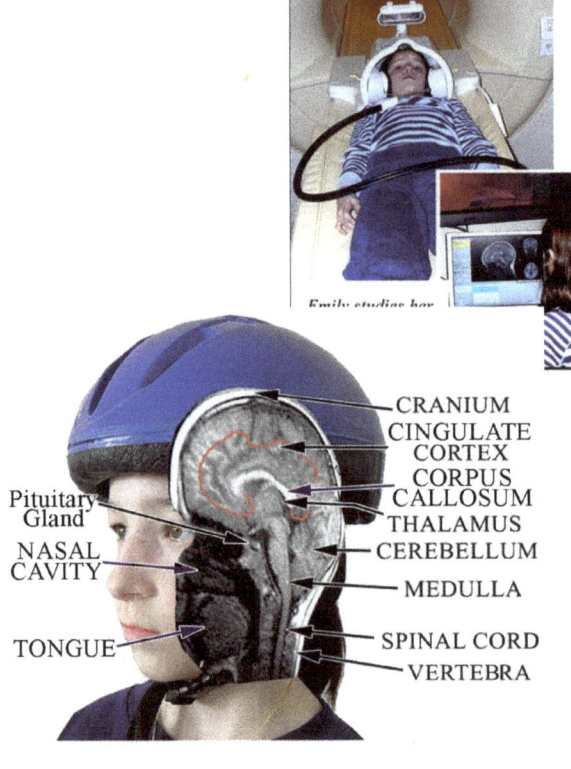

What is magnetic resonance imaging that is used by most studies discussed in this book? It is a response of atomic nuclei of the brain to radio waves when placed in a strong magnetic field to produce brain images. These pictures show my daughter Emily in the scanner with a head coil on that improves brain signals (left). On the right I stripped away the plastic cover to show that the main part of the scanner is a huge magnet. The vibrations one hears in the scanner are produced by electrical currents passed through the magnet and are partially muted with ear plugs.

We begin with a brief overview by looking at the middle of Emily's brain coregistered with a picture of her head for orientation; we are looking at her right hemisphere in this picture. The bone that protects the brain is called the cranium and the red outlined area is cingulate cortex which surrounds the front, top and back of the corpus callosum (labelled "CC" in the next and subsequent pictures). The corpus callosum is white and is composed of axons that connect both hemispheres. There are many parts to cingulate cortex but we will only consider two divisions of anterior cingulate cortex (subgenual, sACC; and pregenual, pACC), two parts of midcingulate cortex (anterior, aMCC and posterior, pMCC), and the dorsal part of posterior cingulate cortex (dPCC). The thalamus lies below the corpus callosum and has connections with the entire cortex including cingulate cortex. Finally, the pituitary gland is shown because it secretes hormones that can be destructive in maltreated adolescents and PTSD.

Youngsters and adults with ADHD do not have normal cingulate cortices as shown on the left four images in the next picture; i.e., those of us with ADHD start our life with brain damage, it can be detected in adults as well and is not reversible. In all images the top and back of the brain was trimmed off to focus attention on cingulate cortex. The right and left hemispheres from Makris and colleagues (2007; *Cerebral Cortex*, volume 17, pages 1361-1325; top two images) show where cingulate thinning in both hemispheres occurs (the most intense yellow is where thinning is greatest). We do not know why the cortex shrinks but it could be due to lose of neurons (brain cells) or their dendrites that look like trees and collect information from other neurons (see the cover photograph showing neuron cell bodies and dendrites emerging from them on my left ear). Atrophy is correlated with impaired thinking shown in the third image on the left from He and colleagues (2015; *Neuroscience Letters*, volume 600, pages 45-49) who studied children and adolescents. Thus, atrophy is thought to be a negative impairment that may explain delayed learning and social capabilities and attention deficits. Finally, connections among areas in the ADHD brain are not the same as for healthy control subjects. The fourth image is from a study of adults with ADHD by Costellanos and colleagues (2008; *Biological Psychiatry*, volume 63, pages 332-337) that shows changes in connections with dPCC. Of particular note is the *reduction* in connections with pMCC (coded in blue) also possibly related to impairments in cognition, attention and hyperactivity. Thus, from the earliest part of my life to this day I have impaired cingulate functions. One should

The ADHD and Abuse-Damaged Brain

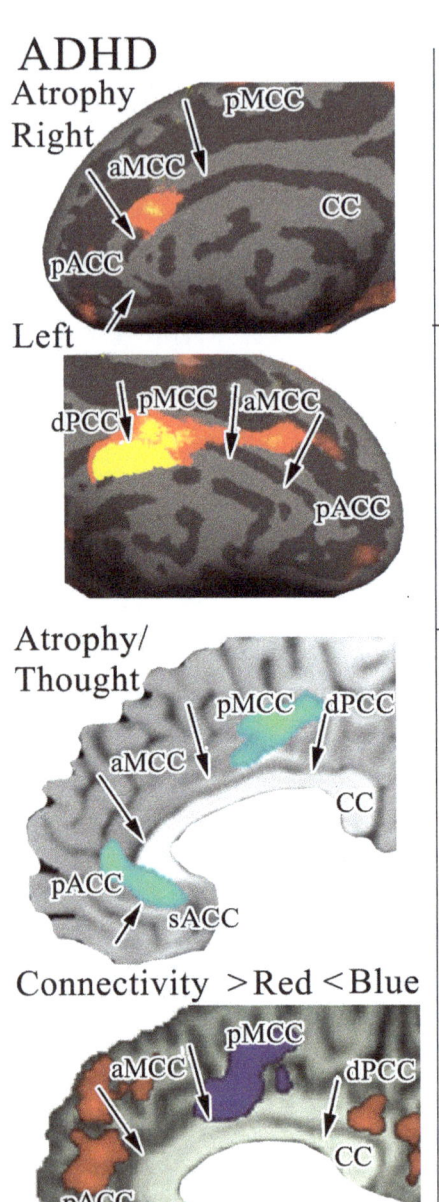
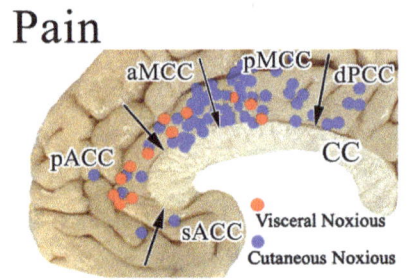
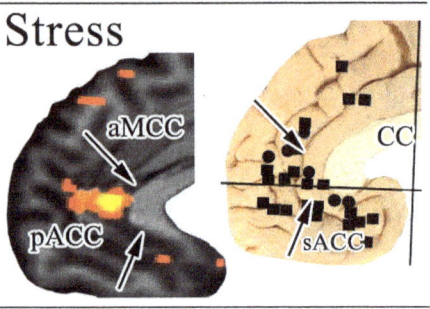
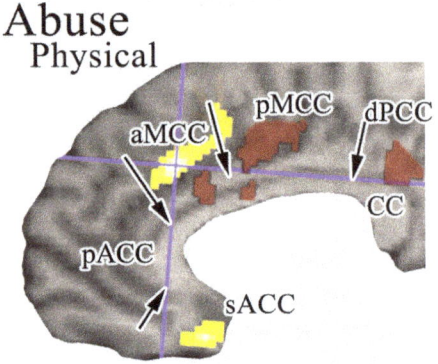
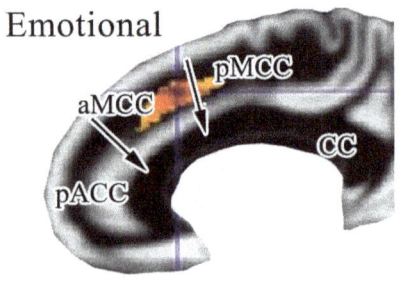

remember we are only looking at part of the story as other areas of the brain are also impaired.

My story does not stop there, however, because my parents layered onto ADHD different forms of pain, stress and abuse, PTSD evolved from it and all combined to seriously damage my MCC and ACC. The four images on the right of the picture below show different types of responses that are often part of abuse be it physical, neglectful or emotional. 1) Noxious (painful) simulation of the skin (cutaneous) such as burning heat or mechanical tweezers mainly activate the spots at the blue dots reported in separate studies (vs responses for single studies as in the left panels). (Yes, people actually lay in the scanner while the investigator does this to them under controlled conditions with approval from the Investigational Review Board for human studies). This image is from one of my studies published in 2005 in *Nature Reviews Neuroscience*. Most of the blue dots are in aMCC but there are also quite a few studies reporting peak activity in the pMCC and very few in dPCC. In contrast, inducing pain in the viscera (colon, stomach or esophagus) with pressure, acid or other noxious compounds evokes activity mainly and proportionately more in pACC and fewer in aMCC as shown with the red dots for each study. Thus, when you are experiencing various forms of short duration noxious stimuli, these are some of the areas in your brain that are active among others. As an aside, we were using an inflatable-balloon stimulator in the esophagus of an experienced technician while he was in the scanner. The balloon exploded, but he did not move; if he had it would have interfered with the study. We removed the collapsed balloon, inserted another and the experiment went on to its conclusion. Now that is commitment to finishing a study!

PTSD occurs in about 20% of people who experienced one or more traumatic events and its severity can depend on age with younger individuals being more vulnerable. PTSD emerges from maltreatment and the right image labeled "Stress" is one in which brain activity was assessed by comparing fearful versus happy facial expressions in a study of PTSD by Shin and colleagues (2005; *Archives of General*

Psychiatry, volume 62, pages 273-281). The activity was in pACC. The adjacent plot (far right) is of many studies also summarized by Shin and colleagues. Most of the marks are located in pACC and sACC. This is the cingulate region that is particularly vulnerable to stress.

The third image in the figure labeled "Abuse/Physical" shows findings from two studies. The first documents mainly shrinkage and excess arousal of the vulnerable part of aMCC (shown in yellow with the blue lines identifying the place of peak shrinkage from a study by Thomaes and colleagues (2010; *Journal of Clinical Psychiatry*, volume 71, issue 12 pages 1636-1644). In another study by Ringel and colleagues (2008; *Gastroenterology*, volume 134, pages 396-404), activity evoked by painful rectal stimulation minus non-painful balloon distension in women that had been raped and physically abused (attacked) multiple times. Responses in this study are coded in red. There are a number of interesting differences in these studies due to study groups, levels of abuse, stimulation sites and parameters but the main takeaway is that both studies show profound atrophy in MCC. Thus, harsh adolescent physical abuse such as beating and rape has a profound impact on cingulate cortex; particularly MCC. Finally, van Harmelen and colleagues (2010; *Biological Psychiatry*, volume 68, pages 832-838) reported that child emotional maltreatment before age 16 but analyzed in adults at ~age 39 showed thinning mainly in aMCC (fourth image on the right in the picture). Shortly we will consider the definitions of abuse in general and as it relates to my upbringing.

A final note is warranted about the components of what is termed the "limbic system." This system deals with many aspects of emotion and memory. The picture here was obtained on the internet from Soton Brain Hub and provides a short overview of this system. The dotted line adds the anterior insula that is also part of the limbic system but is not on the medial surface.

A Short Lesson in Cingulate Neuropathology

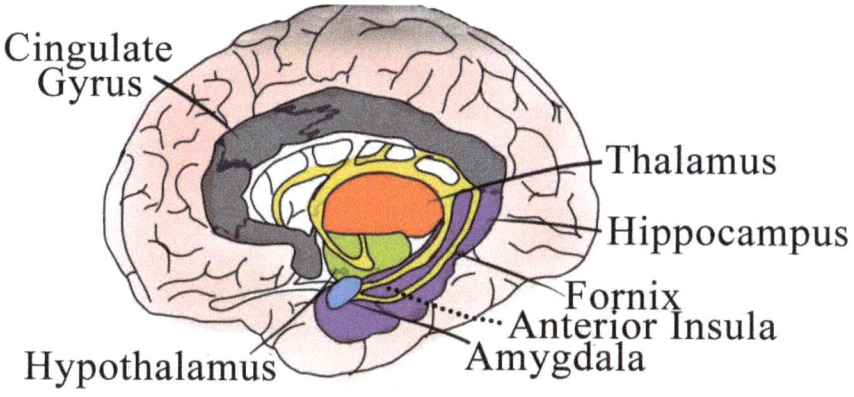

This system is involved in various aspects of emotion, memory and autonomic (automatic reflex) and conditioned behaviors. It is also termed "The Emotional Brain" and references to emotion throughout this volume refer specifically to this system. Also, when it is stated herein that cingulate cortex is not the only structure involved in particular functions, these are the additional sites that may be so engaged. For example, the amygdala is heavily involved in fear not just MCC. The hypothalamus receives input from cingulate cortex and controls hormonal responses via the pituitary gland during stress and the hippocampus is engaged in most forms of short-term memory including that for emotion.

There! You have had the shortest lesson in cingulate neuroanatomy and neuropathology ever given. I hope you see how important and vulnerable this region is to ADHD, pain, stress and multiple forms of abuse. Its vulnerabilities may also be expressed in the important dichotomy of vulnerable and resilient individuals and the level of depression and anxiety experienced by patients. One can reasonably conclude that as more forms of abuse and ADHD accumulate damage in the brain, there is a radical reorganization of circuits and functions referred to as brain plasticities. Apparently my brain has all of these deformities and there is no chance that they can be currently reversed.

Once you lose a neuron, it is gone forever, although we can compensate to some extent with those that remain.

VIGNETTE
3

Attention-Deficit/ Hyperactivity Disorder

AFTER WE DEFINE issues relating to ADHD, we will consider how this disorder impacted my entire life. ADHD is not a form of abuse but there is a high link between the two. According to Sanderud and colleagues (2016; *European Journal of Psychotraumatology*, volume 7, article 32061), child maltreatment is associated with higher levels of ADHD symptoms in young adults. Co-occurring (multiple) types of maltreatment display stronger associations with ADHD symptoms with attenuated effects for sexual abuse and males confer stronger associations with ADHD symptoms than females. Individuals in the abused group reported the highest number of ADHD symptoms, suggesting that individuals in this class have a higher probability of developing ADHD in later life. This may be due to the severe nature and number of types of abuse in this group that induce negative outcomes. Thus, ADHD has a 2-3 times higher rate when a history of childhood abuse is present (see the double arrow in the second picture in Vignette 1). Critically for my life, the authors note that the behavioral patterns of children with ADHD symptoms may elicit emotionally abusive responses from caregivers; they certainly did from my parents.

The association of these two syndromes can be documented in my life as ADHD generated behaviors that my parents found unacceptable for a Christian boy and they tried to beat them out of me. It is a critical part of my Lifeline, the source of my physical abuse and it has been part of my entire life. Before addressing my specific experiences in terms of ADHD, it is appropriate to enumerate some of its symptoms and consider a hypothesis about why its genetic predisposition is so highly conserved in the human population with a reported frequency of 10-30%, tends to run in families and is associated with child maltreatment. This high percentage of expression in humans assures that many reading this book live with it as well.

ADHD is a neurodevelopmental problem that runs high in children and adolescents and usually lingers into adulthood. It is associated with attention deficits, hyperactivity, delayed cognitive performance and social interactions. Adults with ADHD may have trouble prioritizing and starting and finishing tasks. They tend to be disorganized, restless, and easily distracted. Some people with ADHD have trouble concentrating while reading. The inability to stay focused and follow through on tasks can derail careers, ambitions, and relationships. Adults also have problems with self-control and this can lead to difficulty controlling anger, impulsive behaviors, and blurting out rude or insulting thoughts. Some have no compunctions in saying things that might be true but will hurt others due to a lack of empathy. So why do ADHD genes linger in the human genome at such a high rate?

One view is that it is simply more frequently diagnosed, and this may be true but does not solve the problem. I contend that its genetic sustainability has valuable functions in human society in adults because difficulties with attention, hyperactivity, impulsivity, social difficulties, and slow cognitive development can be overcome to some extent in adulthood with early parental guidance, psychotherapy and/or the drugs Ritalin and Vyvanse. Some well-known individuals have discussed their ADHD and how it affects their adult career development. 1) Michael Phelps is a 22-time medaled Olympic swimming champion that was diagnosed with ADHD at age 9. If he didn't want to read, his mother gave him the sports page from the newspaper. She encouraged him to swim, which he says helped him develop concentration and self-discipline. 2) Howie Mandel is a comedian, actor, and TV host who says that living with ADHD made for a tough childhood and adulthood. Mandel didn't earn his high school diploma, but says his parents and wife have always been supportive. His ADHD and obsessive-compulsive disorder are part of his comedy. 3) James Carville is a political analyst and commentator who was diagnosed with ADHD in his late 50s. He went to be checked at the urging of his wife, who said he couldn't sit still or pay attention. He says, "I have been fortunate enough that I have a structure around me that I have built over a period of time to deal with it." 4) Katrina Smirnoff is a "Dancing With the Stars" professional dancer who says that when she was young, her parents helped by giving her many outlets for her hyperactivity. She was involved in ballet, figure skating, playing the piano, and gymnastics. As an adult, she credits medication for helping her stay focused and organized during busy days. Finally, Terry Bradshaw is a Super Bowl champion and TV sports commentator says ADHD made him struggle in school and so he put more effort into sports. Now an author and motivational speaker, he talks openly about his ADHD and how he is able to control his symptoms with medication. There are, of course, many other examples. Thus, those of us with ADHD can overcome its deficiencies with parental guidance, psychotherapy and medication to become very successful adults.

There are as many as 62 possible genes playing a causative role in ADHD (Kline and colleagues, 2017; *Neuroscience and Behavioral Reviews*, volume 80, pages115-155). However, environmental factors have been identified that may evoke it or interact with some genes. While parental attachment issues were clearly a problem for me, I know of no other environmental factors that induced my ADHD; e.g., Blanche did not smoke including during her pregnancy, exposure to neurotoxins like pesticides also were unlikely. They are briefly mentioned here as they could be relevant to the reader and/or their children. ADHD links to environmental factors have been demonstrated for a number of risk factors and the following conclusions are formulated in various articles. 1) Children born to mothers who bore their first child early in their reproductive lives are at increased risk of ADHD. 2) Prenatal smoking enhances the risk for ADHD. 3) Parental attachment problems and environmental factors are associated with childhood ADHD. Adults with ADHD have a much higher incidence of insecure attachment styles than in the general population. For example, I still do not easily form long-term friendships. 4) Clusters of ADHD could be related to some environmental variables such as exposure to pesticides, organochlorine compounds and air pollutants because of traffic around the living environment. These were not exposures for me.

How do I know that I had and have ADHD even when it went unrecognized 65 years ago? ADHD is currently identified with parent and teacher questionnaires such as the Vanderbilt ADHD Parent Rating Scale. Reports of a few of my elementary school teachers point to the fact that I did indeed have ADHD symptoms. One teacher reported in 1954, "Brent made a slow start in reading but is improving. He is *inattentive* during the reading periods and does not always do his best. He frequently interrupts the class and bothers the children near him. His writing needs improvement for he is careless and *hurries* too much with his written papers. His number work is poor and not satisfactory. Brent's attention toward his school work needs to improve. He is too much inclined to be *inattentive and careless.*" In 1955 (2nd grade) another teacher reported, "Brent shows a *serious lack of social adjustment. His behavior pattern is that of a much younger and immature child.* This, of course, affects his work in the classroom…. His *emotional instability has had a retarding effect on his reading ability.* As soon as Brent begins to develop some measure of self-control and a more thoughtful attitude towards others I feel sure that he will find his school work improving." In 1958 it was said, "Brent often *acts impulsively and erratically too secure attention…* Applied spelling is very weak and reading is jerky."

It is clear from these reports that my school work and social adjustment were delayed as would be expected in an adolescent with ADHD. Moreover, as an adult I took the Vanderbilt Rating Scale both before and after starting chewing nicotine gum. The latter activity arose for me as I wondered why individuals with ADHD engage in a high level of smoking. One explanation could be that they self-medicate with nicotine to improve their cognitive performance. Therefore, I started chewing nicotine gum and sure enough I was able to focus more effectively on tasks such as writing this book. Interestingly, I fully qualified for ADHD on the Vanderbilt Scale before but not after taking this medication. Finally, the presence of ADHD in my daughter, who was diagnosed with current instruments, has this disorder and further supports the view that I also have it due to its highly genetic (familial) nature.

Details of ADHD symptoms in adults. Many adult tasks necessary for success in everyday life are dull; from making a grocery list to filling out documents at work. People with ADHD tend to put off boring tasks in favor of more enjoyable activities. In people with ADHD, brain chemicals called neurotransmitters are less active in areas of the brain that control attention and thought including cingulate cortex. Researchers don't know exactly what causes this chemical imbalance(s), but genes likely play a role as noted above. Studies have also linked ADHD to prenatal exposure to cigarette smoke and alcohol.

Many adults don't learn that they have ADHD until they get help for another problem such as anxiety or depression. Discussing poor habits, troubles at work, or marital conflicts often reveals that ADHD is at fault. To confirm the diagnosis, the disorder is usually present during childhood, even if it was never diagnosed. Old report cards or talking with relatives can document these issues as they did for me. Coping with the symptoms of adult ADHD can be frustrating in itself. At the same time, many adults with ADHD struggle with depression, anxiety, and/or obsessive compulsive disorder. They're also more likely to smoke or abuse drugs.

ADHD in adults can sabotage marriages and other relationships such as those in committees and other professional activities. The condition makes it difficult to remember social commitments, birthdays, or anniversaries, finish household chores, and pay bills on time. Adults may lose their tempers easily or engage in reckless behavior (e.g., my experiences as a "Boston driver"). This leads to higher rates of separation and divorce. I was reprimanded for forgetting my wife's 60th birthday but fortunately she is forgiving and did not divorce me for it. Adults with ADHD usually do not outgrow the condition but may learn to manage it successfully in these circumstances as noted above for some well-known patients. Holding a job can be difficult and they often have trouble breaking down tasks into manageable parts and following directions, staying organized and meeting deadlines. They are also prone to tardiness and careless mistakes. In one national survey, only half of adults with ADHD were employed full time, compared to 72% of adults without the disorder. People with ADHD also tend to earn less than their peers.

Beyond the well-recognized symptoms of ADHD, I would like to make three observations about my behavior that I term core deficiencies that are related to these symptoms (the first is a symptom) and might be considered in adolescents with ADHD and/or abuse-damaged brains. These help characterize specific problems that may be associated with ADHD and/or its combination with the abuse-damaged brain: 1) impulse/urge control, 2) lack of recognizing boundaries, and 3) substantially reduced fear of threatening situations all of which may be due to severe damage to MCC as well as other parts of the brain.

Impulse/urge control is a core deficiency and symptom of ADHD. A common feature of ADHD is reflected in deficits in urge (impulse) control that is organized in MCC but is damaged in ADHD. Impulse control deficits can interfere with activities of daily living in ADHD and are chiefly associated with actions that cannot be realized immediately and must be held in check until an appropriate time and context when they might be released. To verify that MCC is relevant to urge control, we consider micturition and its role in the urge-for-action. In these experiments the bladder is catheterized and precisely filled to the point of the urge-to-urinate. When we become aware of having a full bladder as done with subjects in an imaging scanner, the urge-to-void must be withheld because we do not void our bladder anywhere, but withhold it until an appropriate *context* is identified. The MCC is activated during this urge and most others. The urges mediated by MCC are encountered in ADHD and include those associated with rushed driving without consideration for traffic laws and consequences, love (kissing and sexual responses), social interactions and professional committee work, some responses of which should be withheld, etc. Thus, one postulate about ADHD is that deficits in urge control are associated with impulsiveness and its psychopathology is mainly due to MCC damage.

Recognizing boundaries; another core deficiency in ADHD. Each of the above symptoms contribute to general behavioral problems and another general one is recognizing and adjusting to boundaries such as my disrupting class activities. Healthy individuals easily learn their personal boundaries including what constitutes the property of others, their role in school and the workplace and the limits thereto, family expectations, the rules of driving defensively and even knowing one's turn and limits in general conversations. One indication of the disorder is finishing someone's sentences before they are done talking. I did not observe any of these boundaries as an adolescent as per a few of the following examples.

1) In grammar school I often acted out by distracting the class from assigned activities. When Blanche arrived on one parent's day at school, she found me sitting in the front corner of the classroom with a dunce cap on (times were quite different then). Needless to say, she was extremely embarrassed by her son's position and this did not enhance my relationship with her.

2) At another time when I was about 12, I took my double-edged axe, which I was quite proud of, into a neighbor's tree to chop off branches as property and property lines had little impact on my behaviors. I also had little fear of such an activity. Blanche's efforts to get me down from high up in the tree took some effort on her part and displeased her greatly.

3) As a cooperative-education student working in financial analysis at Exxon (then Esso) in Linden, NJ, I found it striking that by simply paying our bills for tankers of oil on time we could save $10,000 for each one. The problem appeared to be with the unionized workers in an adjacent room that held up the invoices. I went to them and asked them to send the invoices to me promptly so the bills could be paid

on time. I was amazed at the reprimand from my supervisor who was on the verge of firing me! I have always had a marginal view of unions since then.

4) Professionally, neuroscience as a discipline is an ideal undertaking for someone who does not recognize mental boundaries. While many neuroscientists worked in individual or pairs of disciplines such as anatomy, physiology, neurology, pharmacology and/or behavioral science, particularly in the early days of neuroscience, I found it quite easy to traverse these "boundaries" and engage in multiple interdisciplinary research activities which continues to this day.

Neuroscience was the ideal format for a young adult with ADHD and a failure to observe predetermined intellectual boundaries. Yes, I was studying for an anatomy degree with the structure and connections of cingulate cortex, however, these connections have functional outcomes that could also be studied with a new method at the time called brain slicing. How exciting to be able to remove thin slices of cingulate cortex and study the excitatory functions of an anatomical connection that I was also studying. I developed the first "callosal slice preparation" that included cingulate cortex in the rat brain. I took thin slices of cingulate cortex including both sides of the brain and the corpus callosum between them, kept them alive in warm salt solutions and stimulated one side of cingulate cortex with electrodes while recording from inside single neurons with very fine glass electrodes on the other side of the brain. How exciting it was to see the first ever recorded intracellular cingulate responses.

5) In another example, I purchased a kayak in my early-20s and was intrigued by the large oil and gas cargo ships in the Boston Harbor. I could not resist (impulsively) paddling my kayak out to one of them anchored in the harbor so that I could look up at this gargantuan ship and touch its rough and eroding hull. I simply had no fear of such an activity; fear is mediated by aMCC that was severely damaged in my brain.

6) My social skills have always been deficient. I once broke my nose playing hockey in high school and the physician laid my head on a bed, held it down with his knee, and cracked my nose back into

place. To this day I have a hole in my nasal septum that allows me to perform a trick which I showed at my son's college graduation dinner. Threading a string through the hole and tying it to a fork, I stood up holding the fork suspended in mid-air. Everyone found this trick quite disgusting and inappropriate. I still do not know why it is perceived as such as it is a continuation of my adult ADHD.

7) Finally, I lived in Boston for about 15 years and have had problems maintaining speed limits when driving and the bad habits of Boston drivers are well known. Either they have a higher incidence of drivers with ADHD or they are too anxious to get to their destination to care about the activities of other drivers. It appears I had the worst combination of risk factors for driving. In one instance, the traffic on the Southeast Expressway was so clogged that I closely followed an ambulance through traffic in a technique called "drafting." The air flow of the ambulance ahead of me pulled my car along. I made really good time but I was an accident waiting to happen.

This last problem with driving is not unique to my experience and is a take-home message for parents and youths with ADHD. It has been reported in a study by the Children's Hospital of Philadelphia that individuals with ADHD are involved in more traffic accidents (crashes), driving while intoxicated, not wearing a seat belt, speeding and lose their licenses more often than their peers.

Thus, failure to understand and recognize boundaries is related to impulsivity and attention deficits which begins early in adolescence and usually continues throughout adult life. It usually does not just go away with maturation and there are drug interventions with Ritalin and Vyvanse at all ages that resolve this problem in the brain; neither drug was available for me when I needed them. Most intriguingly, this symptom of lacking boundaries probably should *not* be treated in adults as it can play a very important and positive role in one's career. As argued below, the genes that contribute to this function can have positive social and cognitive value; not just negative ones.

Pushing boundaries as an adult can be very risky and has a high cost as one butts heads intellectually with entrenched principles as in my experience with scientific endeavors. The late Dr. John Silber, past president of Boston University was an important thought leader, who said, "One can forget the meaninglessness of his own existence by occupying himself with scientific experiments of dubious import. Countless scientists and scholars spend their lives in the search of truths that are irrelevant to them." He also said, "it was the duty of a leader to change the world to their views rather than simply confirm the beliefs of others. The goal of a leader is to change the way people view their science; not to compromise with them for financial gain but rather to force change and improve the human condition." The same views can be applied to business, art or any other life endeavor. The Silber statements sound strikingly like involving the core issue of crossing boundaries by adults with ADHD; ones that carry the ADHD individual to new endeavors in science, art and business. In other words, these genes have positive benefits.

Healthy individuals can understand the value of "thinking "outside the box." However, it appears to be a struggle for them to achieve such a goal as their life begins early with the definition of their boxes and living to avoid confrontation by staying therein. Various approaches to career development include going beyond your "comfort zone" and trying to think out of the box. Amazingly, as individuals with ADHD do not recognize boundaries in the first place, we naturally live outside the boxes determined for us by society. My entire scientific career was

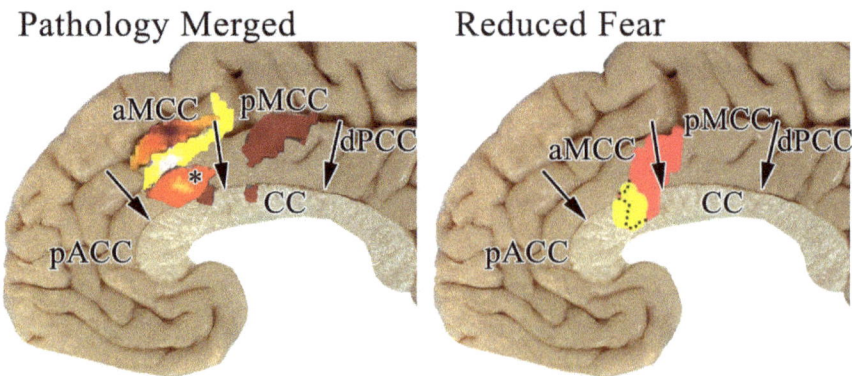

spent outside predefined boxes. The National Institutes of Health (NIH) want to support innovative research but the committees that evaluate grant applications are comprised of generally normal, academically accomplished and high achieving individuals who live and work in their respective boxes. When they are presented with grant applications that are truly innovative, they often do not understand how to analyze and support them. The relevant issues do not seem to make sense to them. Hence, the notion that the NIH can support truly innovative research is often not realized. Many reviewers default to new methods and quantitative accounting details that make little progress toward qualitatively important progress in science as per Dr. Silber's quote ("The goal of a leader is to change the way people view their science; not to compromise with them for financial gain but rather to force change and improve the human condition").

Reduced fear responses. A third core deficit in ADHD is an inability to respond to threatening situations. The above list of seven examples of my crossing boundaries has an underlying suggestion that we do not have intact fear responses; for example, not fearing disciplinary actions in the classroom (1, above), climbing into a tree with a double-edged axe (2), imposing on unionized workers (3), approaching and touching an oil tanker hull in Boston harbor from a small kayak (5), social stigmas (6), offensive and dangerous driving (7). Finally, as in the later Vignette 12, I describe a time when I intervened in a fight between a man and a woman on the subway, while others simply stood or sat by and watched; once again showing my lack of fear to the consequences of my behavior to help this woman.

We can account for my lack of fear responses to threatening situations by the damage produced by ADHD and its combination with abuse in the brain; here we emphasize cingulate cortex but other areas are also involved in impaired fear responses including the amygdala. This illustration has two parts. In the first (left) I have merged pathologies shown in the third figure in Vignette 2 with the asterisk identifying shrinkage associated with ADHD and the other three sites with shrinkage due to abuse. The greatest damage (lose of neurons, dendrites and/

or axons) is in aMCC. Based on these observations, this structure is very dysfunctional in my brain. In the second picture (right) there are sites associated with reduced threat responses; i.e., avoidance of electrical shock to the skin. The yellow site is from Spenser and colleagues (2017; *Psychiatry Research: Neuroimaging*, volume 262, pages 55-62) and the second coded in red is from Maier and colleagues (2014; *Psychological Medicine*, volume 44, pages 85-98). Both sites overlap at the dotted line and their extension into the corpus callosum (CC) is likely a technical artifact (i.e., it should be in the cortex not the corpus callosum).

Fear is something we use to avoid threatening objects and situations and these two early studies suggest that mainly aMCC damage reduces these responses. Thus, while a reduction in fear is not an established symptom of ADHD and/or abuse, this impairment may be a critical part of these syndromes. More such studies will likely continue to focus attention on this problem in the ADHD and abuse-damaged brain as well as MCC.

ADHD: A successful human variant NOT necessarily a disorder: Use it! As already noted, there are many genes linked to ADHD and likely more will be discovered. The conundrum here is that we consider these individuals to have a "disorder" and as such one would expect that if the genes and associated behaviors have no value, they would over time (millennia) be expected to disappear from the human genome. I have argued so far that at least in adults various ADHD symptoms can be employed to useful ends as also shown in other successful individuals noted above and we might *not* expect these genes to disappear as they construe competitive advantages on the individuals that bear them. Some adults with ADHD can focus intently on things they enjoy or find interesting - the ability to hyper-focus, but they struggle to pay attention to tasks that bore them.

One genetic variation that causes ADHD-like traits is more common in the world's nomadic peoples. Researchers think that traits such as impulsive behavior, novelty-seeking, and unpredictability might have helped nomads track down food and other resources. So the same qualities that make it challenging to excel at a desk job may have been an advantage to our nomadic ancestors.

Recent studies have clarified many aspects of the ADHD syndrome in terms of academic performance. Test anxiety, test performance, psychological stress and the hormone cortisol reactivity to stress in adults with ADHD compared with healthy controls was assessed by Raz and Leykin (2015; *Psychoneuroendocrinology* Vol 60, pages 7-17; see this article for validation references). Participants with ADHD had significantly higher baseline levels of Cognitive Obstruction test anxiety, Tenseness test anxiety and Total test anxiety. Individuals with ADHD tend to perceive test situations as more threatening than those without it. Anxiety disorders are a common comorbid condition (simultaneous presence of two or more conditions) among individuals with ADHD with a prevalence ranging from 15-35%, and even reaching as much as 50% depending on a study's sample population. College students with ADHD report higher total test anxiety and suggest other aspects of test anxiety, including worry and emotionality.

Thus, there are significant differences between ADHD and non-ADHD students regarding their perceptions of and anxiety during test taking. Those with ADHD perceive themselves as having more difficulty in reading under timed conditions and report more test-related anxiety than their peers. Adults with ADHD often demonstrate academic difficulties that result in lower grades than peers and less academic success overall. On a personal note, let me say that while I did very poorly in 7th grade (mostly Ds), this changed significantly in my senior year when I received mostly Bs. Although I was the first in my family to go to college and received very poor advice in this regard, when I identified the joy of learning in my second undergraduate experience, I was able to focus on my studies and graduated *cum laude* (with honors).

I too had comorbid ADHD and an anxiety disorder, although I did not realize it at the time and in university I was able to overcome test taking anxieties and became quite proficient at test taking. My solution guaranteed an A on each exam thus reducing my anxiety. My strategy involved the following steps: 1) Take very careful notes in class. 2) Two weeks before an exam, divide the notes into ~12 equal parts. 3) On the first night of studying, memorize what you can of the first pages. 4) On the second night re-write the notes from the first night as best as one can and try to memorize the next group of pages. 5) This was repeated for about a dozen nights and by the end I could rewrite the entire course notes from memory. 6) Go into the exam, turn the paper over and write down the essential parts of all the notes. 7) Turn the paper over and take the exam with reference to the notes. This approach worked every time because the professor was limited to asking questions about his lecture! You were almost always guaranteed an A and this resolved my test taking anxiety. You or your child with ADHD may be able to contrive an approach like this to resolve test-taking anxiety. Taking multiple practice tests with parental encouragement may also be helpful.

The focus and challenges of neuroscience in graduate school further *improved* my ability to learn course materials and achieve a much better learning experience. In other words, the symptoms of ADHD can be ameliorated when the conditions are right for individual achievement; i.e. activities that consumed my interest. My social skills and impulsivity, however, have never reached levels comparable to my peer abilities and these factors have dogged me for my entire career and I attribute them to a lack of empathy as to what my various colleagues had for expectations and often unwillingness to bend to their desires and expectations.

As already noted, the most common medicines for ADHD are stimulants such as Ritalin (methylphenidate) and Vyvance. This appears ironic for restless or hyperactive people. However, and I speak from some experience with my daughter, these drugs appear to sharpen concentration and curb distractibility by affecting attention networks in the brain and she developed better reading skills. Studies have shown adults taking stimulants have fewer ADHD symptoms - and some people may feel they can concentrate better within about 30 minutes. It is also an interesting observation that patients with ADHD smoke more than the general population. As already noted, it is my hypothesis that they smoke for the nicotine that helps them focus attention on a particular task but the tradeoff of cancer risks is high. Their willingness to take this risk could be due to a lack of fear, foresight or simply not considering other options. In contrast, I started chewing nicotine gum to improve cognition rather than smoke which I have not done for 40 years. I am chewing it right now and bite off a 1 milligram piece every half hour or so to keep my level of attention and focus high. One might try this approach to resolving some ADHD symptoms with the reservation that nicotine is an addictive substance and I have found that, upon starting the day, it can occasionally evoke intestinal motility requiring defecation.

Given all the above noted deficits, including many from which I suffered, why is it possible to state that these symptoms can be ameliorated over time and used in a positive way as adults? One theory posits that ADHD genes conferred a competitive advantage for individuals with them. This is the inverse of current thinking that assumes differences from "normal" behavior are aberrant. While it is justified to provide psychological, educational and pharmaceutical support, this does not mean that we are attempting to produce a normal, healthy individual; the brain is too deformed for this pursuit. These are very important points for parents trying to understand and help their children. The goal is not to change but rather to guide. Not to guide them to becoming "normal" adults but rather guiding them to emerge as their own individual with unique talents and approaches to their life decisions and challenges. Your children do not have a "disorder" and should not be expected to become "normal" according to current socially acceptable standards. Let us take a long (real long) step back in time to better understand the value of the ADHD genes.

Out of Africa. The cradle of human civilization is thought to be in the Rift Valley of Eastern Africa including Ethiopia. Skeletal remains suggest that our ancestors arose about 6-7 million years ago. Although the transition between *Homo erectus* and subsequent *Homo sapiens* (our current species) is still debated, the most accepted theory suggests that *Homo sapiens* differentiated from *Homo erectus* in Africa. It is speculated that *Homo sapiens* migrated at around 60,000-70,000 years ago out of Africa to replace local and more primitive populations in Europe driven by their unique genetic makeup of ADHD-related genes. But wait! Why does this matter in the life of a man or woman in New England or anywhere else in the United States for that matter? The theory as to why the ADHD genes have been conserved is its evolutionary value to the human species that may have driven European explorers around the world including to the Americas. During the 19th Century "Out of New England and other eastern states" could have been the mantra. During the past 100 years "Out to California" could have been invoked by those seeking gold, furs and land with a great climate.

*The **value** of ADHD in modern society.* Having proposed the above theory, we are in a position to consider the context in which to understand a child or adult with ADHD today with unique capabilities and methods of coping. This suggests a continuing and pivotal role for these genes in human behavior. But why exactly do they persist as the entire globe has been populated by humans and there is no need for global exploration? These children seem to have few social and educational advantages over other children; socially they are slow to adapt and recognize social feedback and can be loners. Educationally, they use emotion to code their learning experiences and this is a very brain inefficient way to learn versus the cognitive learning strategies that employ language and mathematics without emotional coding. But these are some of the negative consequences of ADHD and we parents need to consider the unique features of our children and how they develop into adults. Focus on issues for learning and their interests that are of value in relation to their own personal experience and needs. Their view often is, if they do not see a personal need to know, then why bother with it much less learn that it is important. In contrast, the normal population absorbs what they can and are told to do in the classroom. Indeed, the child with ADHD has little interest in being normal at all and will stand and argue for their unique perspectives and goals. My daughter, for example, was taking trumpet lessons in middle school and we would play duets. However, she had a specific approach to the duet that interfered with our playing together. Eventually we had to stop them entirely as she could not conform to playing with me.

The *evolutionary advantage* of the many ADHD genes shows itself once these children have identified their strengths and weaknesses, and are ready to use them to competitive advantage in the adult world where they will compete with healthy individuals. As adults, these children emerge as leaders because they are bored quickly with redundancy and repetition. They seek unique experiences just as they did in the Rift Valley and move forward to explore new ideas and ways of solving problems. They are the ultimate thinkers "out of the box" because they do not accept boundaries or the box(es) that society might attempt to place them in. It is often impossible to get normals to think out of the box and this is reflected in corporations where the healthy normals simply continue to do what they were trained to do. The consequences? General Motors is a good example as for 40 years the normals drove the company into the ground failing to innovate and compete until bankruptcy was the only solution. Healthy individuals can also be negative in the pursuit of science as innovation is hampered by the fact that they usually outperform the slow progress of individuals with ADHD, the former of who make it through the educational system more quickly and efficiently. This is part of the reason why it is difficult to evoke innovation and why technical innovation becomes so important in science. Conceptual innovation requires truly out of the box thinking where paradigm shifts are required. There is a place for every adult with ADHD in our society often as entrepreneurs.

Healthy normals find comfort in repetition as it reassures their beliefs and reduces potential conflicts. Religious services entail a high degree of repetition to the point of repeating mantras including singing the same hymns and reading the same texts over and over. Scientists are generally selected early in high school and tend to be normal due to the early requirements of conformity to a scientific education/

established dogma. As ADHD individuals emerge slowly in a scholastic environment, they are often relegated to non-scientific careers as they have not yet fully gained an understanding and control of their unique cognitive capabilities. Moreover, individuals with ADHD hate repetition and find sitting in religious services engaging in constant mantras to be very difficult much less sitting still for 30 minuates-1 hour. This was certainly my experience.

ADHD in females. My experience as a male requires a note on how girls respond to ADHD. Girls with ADHD appear to experience unique symptoms including self-injury (cutting without intent of death; Swanson and colleagues (2014; *Journal of Child Psychology and Psychiatry* vol. 55, pp 505-515). Rates of suicide attempts and non-suicidal self-injury such as cutting and burning peak in adolescence and early adulthood; females and individuals with other psychiatric symptoms such as those for Borderline Personality Disorder (BPD) appear to be at particular risk of this behavior and it is highly comorbid with ADHD. Young women with histories of childhood ADHD diagnoses report higher rates of suicide attempts and non-suicidal self-injury than non-diagnosed, comparison women. The analyses in a longitudinal study by Swanson and colleagues aimed to examine, with respect to both aspects of self-harmful behavior, (a) ADHD subtype differences and effects of diagnostic persistence (vs. transient and non-diagnosed classifications) and (b) potential effects of impulsivity and comorbid psychopathology ascertained during adolescence. Young adult women with a childhood diagnosis of ADHD-Combined type (hyperactive and inattentive ADHD versus inattentive or hyperactive alone subgroups) were at highest risk for suicide attempts and the most varied and severe forms of non-suicidal self-injury compared with those with ADHD-Inattentive type; participants with a persistent ADHD diagnosis into adulthood were at higher risk than those with a transient diagnosis or those never meeting criteria for ADHD. During adolescence, an objective measure of impulsivity plus comorbid externalizing symptoms such as physical aggression, disobeying rules, stealing and destroying property, occurred simultaneously in the childhood ADHD-young adult non-suicidal self-injury group. Adolescent internalizing symptoms (e.g., depression and anxiety) emerged as a partial mediator of the childhood ADHD-young adult suicide attempt linkage. Thus, ADHD in females, especially when featuring childhood impulsivity and especially with persistent symptomatology, carries a high risk for self-harm. Psychiatric comorbidity with BPD and response inhibition are important to this clinical longitudinal association. My daughter showed me how important these linkages were in her adolescence.

Suicide. Suicide, of course, is not only a female problem; this issue is raised here along with suggestions for how to deal with a child that ideates committing it. I was a suicide risk during the transition years in my early 20s and it was a result of my ADHD, abuse and PTSD experiences and trying to define a new person that had been hollowed out by rejecting my strict religious upbringing. The suicide rate among young Americans aged 10-24 years old soared 56% between 2007 and 2017, according to data released from the Centers for Disease Control and Prevention (October, 2019). "Significant increases were noted in all age groups, but were higher in adolescents 12-17 years old," it said. The rise coincided with the Spring and Fall semesters of school, and dipped during the Summer, suggesting that issues are compounded by anxiety in school when test taking anxiety is frequent and bullying is more likely. Younger children who died by suicide more often experienced relationship problems with family members and friends and less often had boyfriend/girlfriend problems or left a suicide note suggested in a study published in *"Pediatrics"* (2018).

The web site www.e.how.com makes suggestions for parents who have a child that threatens suicide whether or not they have ADHD. 1) Be aware of what constitutes a threat. A child could directly say that they wished they were dead but they could be indirect and make comments like "if I weren't here…" or "…better off without me." They could have self-destructive behaviors that put them in danger. 2) Monitor for some of the early warning signs. Children have fewer life skills for dealing with severe stress. Depression, being picked on or ridiculed, suicide of a person close to them, or feeling socially isolated can all put children at higher risk for suicide and be some of the features of ADHD. 3) Take all threats seriously. You can never take a threat too seriously as you are going to be in a better place knowing that you overreacted than you will be knowing that you were wrong and did not get your child the help they needed. 4) Respond immediately with direct monitoring and connection to professionals; do not let them be alone until you contact a professional. If they are attending school, let the school counselor know. 5) Talk to your child. Do not judge them by labeling their feelings or intentions or assuming "why" they would say or do something. Instead, let them know how much you love them and ask them what is happening. Ask them why they said what they did and what they meant. Be direct and ask them if they have ever tried to hurt themselves or if they would do so. 6) If they do not open up to you, see if they will open up for another close relative or adult. The main thing is not who they talk to, it is that they talk to someone and you know what is happening to them. If they are being socially isolated or bullied, be their advocate and put an end to it. 7) Finally, know where to go for help. Call 911 if your child is in immediate danger. You can also contact your local mental health facility so they can connect you to emergency services.

It should be noted that parental discipline itself such as emotional abuse or neglect can trigger self-harm (cutting more frequently observed in girls than boys) and thoughts of suicide. The above suggestions should come with the proviso that parents have thoroughly engaged in introspection about disciplining their children and are not themselves generating an abusive environment through neglect or emotional maltreatment that are more difficult to define than overt physical abuse as discussed in the next vignette.

Summary and suggestions. It is clear that ADHD is mainly genetic but is also influenced to some extent by aging and environmental factors including abuse. It usually appears in adolescence and continues throughout life with some amelioration. In addition to attention and impulsivity deficits, lack of recognizing boundaries and reduced fear also characterize the disorder. Its symptoms can be reduced to some extent by early Ritalin or Vyvanse therapy to help adolescents cope with it. An important message for older adolescents with ADHD is the serious problem with poor driving habits that need to be consciously overcome in concert with parental supervision. They cannot be simply put on the road with driving instructors like their peers. They need an additional level of counselling to deal with their unique symptoms when driving.

Another important take-away message is that adolescents and adults report success with Vyvanse, although I have no experience with this drug, Emily does. Adults need to modify family, work and other social behaviors usually with the assistance of Behavioral-Cognitive Therapy. As one's life progresses, ADHD symptoms can be used in a productive way professionally as I and others have done. Seeking to push the boundaries of science, art, business and sports, exploring avenues of new social and artistic expression and not complacently following group thinking are just some examples of the value of adult ADHD. As I have aged and watched others deal with ADHD, it is apparent that we can turn the table on this "disorder" rather than become a victim of it. Use your "deficits" to their advantage.

VIGNETTE 4

What is Abuse, Frequency and Consequences?

ALTHOUGH I GREW up in a middle class family where violence was not part of a low socioeconomic environment, my parents had a misconceived notion of how to discipline their children that they thought was based on Biblical teaching. Blanche would routinely hit me on the head and was emotionally neglectful, while Stanley beat me with his leather belt to the point of bleeding in order to avoid sparing the "rod." Blanche was also withdrawn and I often said that it would have been better had I not had a mother at all as her neglect was palpable. As a Fundamentalist Christian family, my parents referred all of our problems to a vague and imperceptible deity. Jesus was presumed to be the personal side of the Holy trinity and prayer was the mechanism by which communication was encouraged. This approach permeated my first 20 years but did not work for me. It is surprising that people who professed such strong religious views could abuse their children for reasons we will explore later.

Let us begin by first defining abuse and its consequences as they are many and can last long into adulthood. Indeed, many of my "brothers and sisters" live in jails, psychiatric institutions, are homeless or spend a marginal social life of suffering without understanding the sources of their torment and behaviors. They often resort to violence, drug abuse and dysfunctional relationships that are compatible with such behaviors. I was fortunate in my 30s to find a therapist, the late

Dr. Marco Alfondary, who helped me crack the wall that was blocking me from the world of relationships; unfortunately, many of my brothers and sisters will not be so lucky as to have such an individual. Many with child abuse-related PTSD enter a life of aggression, drug abuse, and the Cycle of Violence in which they abuse and sexually assault or emotionally abuse the next generation of adolescents.

Here we briefly consider the broader issues experienced in populations as we must agree on what constitutes abuse and how it might influence the situations of particular readers. While generalizing from individual cases provides a means of accessing the broader literature, be it popular or scientific, population-based statistics need to be interpreted with care. For example, women who were raped as children and adolescents frequently develop irritable bowel syndrome (IBS); however, that does not mean that all women with IBS have been raped.

What is child physical, neglectful and emotional abuse? It is still difficult to compare abuse among individuals as it can vary by age, brain vulnerabilities, onset, intensity, frequency, duration and context. The goal of abuse classification is to determine the extent of damage for each type of maltreatment to assist mental health professionals and the justice system in assessing treatment levels and predict likely outcomes just as one would rank burn damage as first, second, or third degree prior to treatment. It is also used for research purposes to define uniform populations of maltreated individuals. Harsh physical abuse cases include relatively frequent injuries such as bruises, welts, burns, abrasions, lacerations, wounds, cuts, bone and skull fractures, and other evidence of physical injury. Rape is a form of physical abuse that, when it is severe and penetrative, involves pain and stress and is experienced as life threatening. Bremner and colleagues (2007; *Journal of Nervous and Mental Disorders,* volume 195, pages 211-218) work with the Early Trauma Inventory-Self Report to classify adolescent trauma (percentages of each category in parentheses) in their sample:

Physical abuse. Slapped in the face (50%); burned with cigarette(s) (9%), punched or kicked (39%), hit with thrown object (23%), pushed or shoved (45%).

Sexual abuse. Touched in intimate parts in a way that was uncomfortable (39%), someone rubbing genitals against your wish (29%), forced to touch intimate parts (26%), someone had genital sex against your will (18%), forced to perform oral sex (15%), forced to kiss someone in a sexual way (14%).

Emotional abuse. Often put down or ridiculed (49%), often ignored or made to feel like you didn't count (41%), often told you are no good (34%), most of the time treated in cold or uncaring way (24%), parents fail to understand your needs (50%).

Litrownik and colleagues (2005, *Child Abuse and Neglect*, volume 29, pages 553-573) measured severity by frequency, chronicity, age of onset, injury, recency, and type. Each child was assigned a severity score from 0-5 on each of five types of abuse: physical, sexual, failure to provide (neglect), lack of supervision, and emotional in the investigator's target ages of 4-8 for the type of abuse, number of children in each category (percentage in parentheses) and average intensity rating. These ratings were based on the subjective meaning of the maltreatment acts to the victim versus objective measures of the maltreatment itself. 1) Physical abuse: 120 (23.1%) score 1.96; 2) Sexual abuse 47 (9.1%) score 3.17; 3) Failure to provide 125 (24.1%) score 2.55; 4) Lack of supervision 140 (27.0%) score 3.06; 5) Emotional abuse 102 (19.7%) score 3.24.

The above studies show that 1) a child's physical abuse severity is related to physical injury (e.g., bruises, cuts, breaks, etc.) that predicts child psychosocial outcomes including internalizing behaviors such as depression and anxiety. 2) Sexual abuse severity is primarily related to the intrusiveness of the perpetrator's behavior (exposure, fondling, penetration) and predicted anger by the survivor. 3) Emotional maltreatment involves restricting a child's movements, denigration by calling them names, ridicule or cursing, threats and intimidation, yelling or screaming (most frequent), rejection. Other non-physical forms of hostile treatment also predicted fewer externalizing and more internalizing problems by the survivors including social withdrawal, suicidal ideation in addition to depression and anxiety. 4) Finally, failure to provide (neglect) refers to the failure of a parent to adequately engage with their children and provide for their development in one or more of the following areas: health, education, emotional development, nutrition, shelter and safe living conditions. Neglect is distinguished from poverty in that neglect can occur only in cases where reasonable resources are available to the family or caregiver. It is related to functioning at the age of 8 for early reported failure to provide supporting the claim that early lapses in providing children with a nurturing and/or adequate environment are likely to have a more profound impact on subsequent functioning.

Beyond the above two studies that tended to emphasize severity, there is also a class of moderate physical abuse. This class includes spanking the buttocks with the hand (~50%) or with an object (~20%), slapped on the face or head (4%), shaking of mainly neonates (9%) or pinching (5%).

Finally, Leserman and colleagues (1996; *Psychosomatic Medicine*, volume 58, pages 4-15) divided physical abuse into beat, hit, or kicked and life-threatening abuse. *Physical abuse involving life-threatening force was the only significant predictor of adult health status* (below). Most brain imaging studies work with individuals that were severely abused to assure they are working with a clearly defined population.

Nonviolent discipline. Straus and colleagues (1998; *Child Abuse & Neglect*, volume 22, issue 4 pages 249-270) consider methods of nonviolent discipline which, of course, are preferred to violent forms of abuse. The Nonviolent Discipline scale they used measures four disciplinary practices that are widely used alternatives to corporal punishment: explanation, time out, deprivation of privilege(s), and substitute activity. It is mentioned here as it provides important alternatives to corporal punishment, the latter of which unfortunately is a matter of course in American society.

Consequences of abuse. These events in childhood and adolescence have numerous long-term effects that have been repeatedly observed in the psychosocial and epidemiological literatures. They include severe emotional and somatic (body) disorders that begin during adolescence and often extend throughout adulthood. Psychiatric changes include substance use disorders such as alcoholism and prescription opioid misuse for self-medication, depression, anxiety and panic disorders, and stress impairments such as PTSD. While the symptoms of these disorders can be found in isolation in some patients, they are often intermixed (comorbid conditions between two or more disorders) because the relevant brain circuits interact in the limbic system. In other words, someone suffering from PTSD is more likely to have depression and self-medicate with alcohol and/or illicit opioids such as oxycodone than healthy individuals who did not have such experiences.

Somatic disorders resulting from abuse include obesity, which can be categorized as a psychiatric condition, and numerous additional disorders. These include chronic pain conditions that last for more than 3 months and are often reported by police officers and military service members with a history of maltreatment as well as women that have been raped. Pain syndromes including fibromyalgia (deep muscle pain), chronic low back pain, gastrointestinal symptoms such as IBS and vulvodynia, headache and migraine, and temporomandibular disorder are commonly associated with child and adolescent abuse.

Early life stress predisposes adults to functional pain (pain for which no organic causes can be identified in a clinic like fibromyalgia) and psychiatric disorders and outstanding among such stressors is child maltreatment. Psychiatric designations include somatization, somatoform disorders, psychogenic disease, and affective spectrum disorders. They are strikingly frequent and it is apparent that functional pain disorders such as fibromyalgia and temporomandibular joint disorder are not always localized peripherally (outside of the nervous system) but may have a "brain-predominant" cause.

Prison inmates. Another outcome of child and adolescent abuse is aggression and violent crime. The Justice Department's Bureau of Justice Statistics reports that women in U.S. prisons reported higher levels of child abuse than women in general. More than 33% of female state prison and jail inmates said they had been abused as children, as did 14% of males. In the general population, estimates of child physical abuse were 12-17% for females and 5-8% for males. For prisoners who had spent part of their childhoods in foster care (recall Antwone Fisher), the abuse rate was higher; 44% of the male and 87% of female prisoners who had spent the majority of their childhood in foster care or institutions reported abuse. This study drew a strong link between prior abuse and violent crime. Among male inmates in state prisons, 76% who were abused and 61% not abused had a current or past sentence for a violent offense. Among female offenders, 45% of the abused and 29% not abused had served a sentence for a violent crime. Due to the high level of adolescent abuse histories in prison inmates, child abusers do not fare well in the penal system as they are more likely to be killed by stabbing. In my instance, I had to consciously abort my urges to kill my parents by engaging in other activities such as brain research that would have a greater importance than their deaths.

Summary and suggestions. We have briefly reviewed the major forms of abuse and considered their consequences in adolescence and adulthood. It is likely that some parents are using moderate physical abuse and emotional abuse without even realizing the long-term consequences they will have on their children including psychiatric and somatic disorders as well as the potential for violent crime. Given the way I was raised, for example, I thought that life-threatening (harsh) physical abuse, which is associated with harmful adult health outcomes, was what I should avoid in my new family. However, I was unaware of the category of emotional abuse. One can only conclude the following: when in a serious emotional state, it is not appropriate for a parent to discipline a child/adolescent. Once rational thought is possible, the nonviolent forms of discipline are the only ones that will not impair their development and have long-term health consequences.

VIGNETTE 5

Parental Histories

THE SEARCH FOR why my parents were capable of harsh physical, neglectful and emotional abuse needs to begin with their upbringing; i.e., the beginning of the Cycle of Violence (Vignette 32). Although this information is scant, there are a few clues. It was reported that my great grandfather Vogt and his family emigrated from Germany through Ellis Island to the Bronx, NY in the late 1890s. As Alsatian (part of France) Germans immigrated to America after 1860 together with thousands of others, I assume they were part of this wave of immigrants. A verification of my background with AncestryDNA showed that I am 64% Germanic European, 29% Eastern European and Russian and 5% English, Welsh and Northwestern European.

My father (Stanley Oscar) was born in 1918 to Oscar Vogt and his wife, neither of whom I ever met, and raised in the decrepit tenement environment of the Bronx in the 1920s-1930s that was populated by Italian, Polish, German and Jewish decedents of Eastern Europe. There were 12 siblings and Stanley was not cared for in a loving family context. The struggles of early 1900 immigrant families in New York City are well known as they sought work and attempted to raise families. Stanley's father was an alcoholic who died at the age of 55; certainly he did not provide a model for parental guidance. The only comment on Stanley's up bringing was that he was "farmed out" to another family that could take care of him more effectively than his birth family. Thus, it is likely that he suffered from neglect and neighborhood violence based on the times, family size, immigrant tenement living and his parent's conditions. The psychologically destructive nature of his upbringing likely set the stage for the Cycle of Violence in our family that he transmitted to me. Indeed, he was in such need of discipline that he enlisted in the National Guard from 1937-1938, the U.S. Army Field Artillery from 1938-1941, and the U.S. Army Air Force from 1941-1945 in the Pacific during World War II where he worked repairing airplanes. He certainly learned discipline in the Army that included doing what he was told by Blanche. These experiences are reminiscent of those of Antwone Fischer, as noted in Vignette 1, who said, "The change for me came through the Navy. It was a really structured environment, which I appreciated. I did well in the Navy…"

Stanley's conversion from Catholicism to the "pure" Bible-based Fundamentalist view likely occurred in New York City after meeting his wife Blanche and before joining the Army. My dutiful father went to church services during his military stint in the Pacific where he reached the rank of Staff Sergeant. Since my parents lived a middle class lifestyle in the 1950s like many others after WWII and Stanley had a stable job at Western Electric in North Andover, MA, we did not suffer from low socioeconomic status that can be associated with child abuse. We will consider each parent in turn to understand the source of their abusive behavior.

Blanche stayed at home to "care" for the children as best she could and I know virtually nothing of her childhood and adolescence that could account for her aggression. Her maiden name was Smith (Schmid or Schmidt in German) and her ancestors likely immigrated to Philadelphia, PA and then moved to the Pennsylvania Dutch (German) region of Pennsylvania where she grew up. Her family was composed mainly of farmers at the time and my uncle Gurney operated a few hundred acre farm where he grew mainly wheat, dairy cows and pigs. Blanche did not discuss her upbringing, although every few years we went to the Pennsylvania Dutch region to visit our relatives on the farm. This appeared to be one of the few activities besides going to church she enjoyed and, given that it is hard to identify family conditions under which she was abused, for this we shall have to resort to her genetics, religious beliefs as prescribed in her view in the Bible and unknown activities in New York City where she met Stanley before WWII.

The Rutherford Grace Church Monthly Herald
June 1950
Brent "Red" Vogt accepts Jesus Christ as Master and Savior!

The angels were singing Glory to His Name in heaven this month as Brent A. Vogt accepted the healing power of Jesus in the Vogt residence in Rutherford.

The three-year old Brent's first memory was of this particular moment in his life.

He approached his mother in the kitchen and expressed the desire that he accept Christ to wash away all of his sins. He knelt in front of the kitchen sink with his mother and prayed fervently for forgiveness for his sins and asked Jesus Christ into his heart.

Praise be to Jesus!

It is unclear how much sinning he had done during the first three years of his life. He was never seen in the Rutherford bars consorting with the local talent and he certainly was not coveting his neighbor's wife as he could not get it up yet. He had not killed anyone, etc. However, according to Biblical teaching, Brent was responsible along with all humanity for the sin of Adam and Eve for getting it on in the Garden of Eden. It is unclear that he actually understood the concepts of sex, sin and murder but apparently that did not prevent him from achieving redemption and satisfying his mother's absurd view that this was necessary at 3.

The good news is that upon dying he will now enter Beulah Land; a very compelling truth for a 3-year old. His mother was thrilled and whenever he had a problem in the future, she sent him to pray to Jesus rather than help him work through difficult emotional and social problems. This was quite convenient for her because her role in child rearing was greatly reduced.

Postscript

It is said that this redemption has a life-time warranty for getting into Heaven. Like all warranties, however, one does not have to exercise it and when Brent gets to the Pearly Gates he will tell St. Peter to go F#%@ himself. In his early 20s, after 2 years studying for the ministry, he rejected Jesus preferring instead to go to hell where all the fun people would be found having casual sex, taking opioids and burning for eternity.

VIGNETTE 6

"Jesus Saves"

WE BEGIN MY story at the tender age of 3 (or 4) with the tongue-in-cheek notice in this newspaper clipping (above; some of which is true). It shows the extent to which Blanche actually believed the Bible word-for-word and her willingness beyond all reason to make it happen for her children. My parents tried the salvation route with me and it failed as I became a diehard atheist, they tried again with my sister and it failed again as she became a Catholic (god forbid; another form of heathenism as far as they were concerned) and once again with my brother. Apparently three times is a charm in the Vogt family as he followed in the prescribed path as an adolescent and later as a teacher at Bob Jones University (BJU) in South Carolina where my parents settled in their final days. My brother Brian had Stanley build him a house so when he died at 91 the 3rd child and his family would get free living for the rest of their lives.

The good son. While we are on a happy note, we should comment on the good son Brian. I never really knew him. In fact, the parents were quite clear that they did not want me to influence Brian and our separation was their intension. He came along as a surprise in the bedroom 9 years after I was born. (Fundamentalists have never quite gotten the sex thing). He slept in a bed across the room from me in the attic and we lived a relatively uneventful life together; I being so much older, we had little in common to share. He was always on the other side of Blanche in church; the strictly enforced seating order was Brian, Blanche, Stanley, my sister Betsy, and Brent. You see, Blanche thought I was a bad influence on Brain and she wanted me to stay as far away from him as I could as part of her sinister master plan to control his environment to produce a better son. This was a critical part of dissociating family bonds.

I refer to Brian as a scientific apologist at BJU because he presents the patina of being a scientist to the Fundamentalists there, while actually being a believer. The difference is that the former requires precise hypotheses and evidence-based thinking, while the latter only requires that one think something is true and therefore it is. According to this viewpoint, the more you believe the more likely it is true. The concept of a god, for example, can be approached scientifically and, as no hypothesis about this entity's existence has been confirmed, their existence scientifically is in serious doubt. At BJU they state, "All courses are taught from a literal six-day recent Creation perspective." Of course, this is an absurd approach in the context of massive contrary evidence from the fossil record, but Brian accepts this as his teaching directive. By focusing on the technical aspects of scientific inquiry, he circumvents atheistic issues and can say that he is teaching his students the scientific method without having to present evidence that a god exists and supports the views of the congregational believers in such a concept. Anyway, he is the good son because he followed in the steps outlined for him by our parents who feared he would be influenced by the elder and bad son.

VIGNETTE 7

Blanche E. Smith (Vogt): A Parental Predator

Abuse from a Stone-Cold Religious Zealot

WHAT ARE THE conditions under which child physical abuse can occur? There are many possible scenarios; a parent with psychopathic tendencies, parents that were raised by a mother that was neglected themselves and do not have the parenting tools to raise their children, stressful life events, or work that takes them significantly away from their children and blocks them from performing their parental duties. Even low socioeconomic status has been linked to physical abuse and neglect. However, as already noted, we lived a middle class lifestyle in the 1950s and, like many others, Stanley had a stable job at Western Electric in North Andover, MA and Blanche stayed at home to "care" for the children. While we discuss Stanley in the next few vignettes, Blanche had no apparent reasons for her physical and neglectful abuse.

She was a stoic and withdrawn woman with few social skills. For her we must consider her abusive instincts as being physical (hitting), projecting her husband's force as a physical abuser onto his children, and one of neglect inspired by Fundamentalist Christianity, stress induced, mother-child relationship problems and possibly genetically based aggression. Indeed, as ADHD is highly genetic and familial, it is quite likely that she had a number of these genes and symptoms herself that she tried to hide but passed on to me.

Blanche was mostly known as a stiff and cold woman. When she made the effort to smile, her lips were usually pursed tightly together and her posture was rigid. She tried on occasion to interact with people when entering and leaving church services and at family gatherings. She did not relate at all with our neighbors in Andover as she practiced the belief that we live in the world but are not of it, i.e., we are isolated from the non-Fundamentalist, social world. There seemed to her to be adequate Biblical justification for dissociating from many of the social activities of the community such as dancing and going to the movies.

Given her cold-hearted approach, it was not surprising that she would confront our problems not with a loving hug and kiss, conversation about a particular issue and possible solutions but rather with neglectful references to asking Jesus to help. "Pray about it" was an often heard solution to personal problems. She was trying to replace the love and warmth of human interactions with praying to Jesus. Jesus is said to be the personal form of god (a third member of the Trinity) that we mortals can understand versus the more abstract deities of the Trinity and in other religions that are aloof and concerned more with the natural universe. Nevertheless, Jesus is thought of as an entity that resides in some way in the "heart" but is also present in interstellar space or beyond.

As a neuroscientist, I view conversations with Jesus and other deities as an interaction between the cortical hemispheres of the brain or on one side of the brain in a system referred to as the default mode network. This latter system is engaged when we are not performing externally driven tasks such as those in school taking a test or at work completing financial or other reports but rather focused introspectively on personal issues. In this interpretation, whether or not god exists is not the question. The belief itself and associated constructs of relevant moralities serves as the basis for guiding decision making in our personal lives. Stanley in particular would spend many hours, open Bible in hand, praying to himself with his default mode network searching for direction in his life. What a poor fool. But we will consider more on him in the next few vignettes.

The religious perspective supporting abuse. My parents were Fundamentalist, Evangelical Protestants. That mouthful is to say, Bible statements are taken at face value and they were encouraged to go into the world and help others find Jesus. Ironically, there are places in the Old Testament that seem to encourage their abuse. Often when we passed a church of another religion on Sundays they would say in a denigrating way, "The true believers." After all, their religious convictions were the only legitimate ones. Their religious zealotry led them to Wednesday evening prayer meetings, Friday choir practice for the children, Saturday youth meetings, Sunday morning church services and Sunday evening church services. If that is not commitment to a religious viewpoint, I do not know what is. If only they had learned of God's love and how to express it.

The Bible in places presents god as tyrannical as in his need for vengeance ("Vengeance is mine, I will repay, says the Lord." Romans 12:19). Many Old Testament texts present harsh chastisements as models for parental correction of children along with assurances of the reality of hell. Proverbs 23:14, states, "Thou shalt beat him with the rod, and shalt deliver his soul from hell." The resulting odd rationale is that the certainty that wickedness will be punished in the hereafter in Hell makes the infliction of pain in the present an act of love; sparing the child of eternal torment. Proverbs 13:14 states, "Whoever spares the rod hates his son, but he who loves him is diligent to discipline him." Stanley would say while he was beating me, "This is for your own good son." He never referred to me as Brent during my beatings. The point here is that our parents actually believed these Old Testament quotes and vigorously put them into action and their Biblical views perverted their concept of love in a family setting. Blanche was quite satisfied with sending Stanley to my bedroom for a beating due to various infractions of her views as to what was appropriate for a Christian boy. Apparently Blanche and Stanley forgot to consider Proverbs 22:6, "Train a child in the way he should go, and when he is old he will not depart from it." This sentence seems to be less harsh but "training" is a concept that is up to interpretation. Also, we might argue over how to interpret the word "rod" above, but that too is not necessary in this context as Stanley interpreted it as using his leather belt. In my early 20s I intuitively recognized that being beaten with any instrument including a leather belt had severe negative effects on me as we shall see.

Maternal aggression. Why was Blanche so aggressive in throwing temper tantrums, verbal and indirect emotional abuse plus physical assault? While Blanche covered her lack of parenting skills and possibly ADHD symptoms with her stoic lack of social interactions, remembering that the isolation of being in the world but not of it enhances aggression, we must still consider briefly why she was so violent, angry and aggressive at times. Although there were 11 siblings in her family and this may have contributed to her not receiving a good model of how to parent her children, I know of no overt abuse as she was tight lipped about her past life; that would be a normal response to child abuse if it occurred. There are, however, well documented instances in which maternal aggression emerges. During lactation aggressive behaviors of the mother are protective to defend their children against danger but with time, this reflex dissipates. This is not the source of Blanche's abuse as it started after the birth of her first two children. As I expressed ADHD behaviors, this is likely one trigger that incensed her anger and violent behaviors.

There are other possibilities the most likely of which could be a genetic predisposition to violent aggression. This subject is too complex to deal with in the current context so I will refer to a few findings of only one study by Veroude and colleagues (2016; *American Journal of Medical Genetics*, Part B, volume 171B, pages 3-43). High risk environments include low maternal sensitivity (Blanche in spades without empathy); impulsivity and anger possibly linked to her ADHD genes; my ADHD if genetic may have been derived from her. The field of genetics is just beginning to confront these difficult problems and it should be remembered that gene-environment interactions including stress add further to the complexity of this problem. However, about 50% of aggressive behavior may be explained by genetic influences. Thus, I hypothesize that one of the fundamental causes of my parent's, particularly Blanche's, aggression and violence was due to their genetic makeup and vigorous religious beliefs. The question then is, how did it express itself in our family?

Spanking children and abuse in the Vogt family. Let me briefly expand on our treatment to the wider views held by many in our society. It is a general consensus in the U.S. that spanking young children is an acceptable form of corporal punishment. As I heard this view expressed by my brother, the question is, is this truly the case with scientific support or is it simply an unsupported belief system as Brian is prone to engage in? I refer to a study by Taylor and colleagues (2010; *Pediatrics*, volume 125:e1057-e1065) in which frequent use of corporal punishment (i.e., mother's use of spanking more than twice in the previous month) when the child was only 3 years of age was associated with increased levels of child aggression when the child was 5 years of age, even controlling for the child's level of aggression at age 3 and other potential confounding features such as socioeconomic status. This study only extended two years following the spanking and we do not know how it affects adolescent or adult behavior. Despite the American Academy of Pediatrics recommendations to the contrary, most parents in the U.S. approve of and have used corporal punishment for child discipline. They, like my brother, apparently do not require scientific facts for guidance. This study suggests that even "minor" forms of corporal punishment, such as spanking, increase the risk for child aggressive behavior. I suspect this is true for me even as an adult; but more about that later. Of course there are alternatives to corporal punishment including nonviolent discipline noted above such as time outs, loss of certain privileges, etc. In my current family we were able to raise two healthy children without corporal punishment.

My sister Betsy adored her older brother and followed him everywhere he went. The adjacent picture captures this relationship very well. One wonders how she felt when observing her older brother being beaten. Let us consider her treatment according to her own words; mine are considered later. Her experiences highlight some aspects of Blanche's poor parenting "skills." My sister witnessed my physical abuse when I was 9 (she is 3 years younger than me). We were living in a boarding house while the Andover, MA house was being built. When the parents decided I needed discipline and in order to not cause a ruckus doing it where we lived, they would take us for a ride on the highway. Stanley would pull the car over and Blanche would make me take down my pants and she spanked my bare buttocks with her hand. Needless to say, this had a negative effect on me and my sister. It appears that even witnessing abuse can have negative consequences.

My sister remembers Blanche hitting me hard on the head with her hand which she did many times and my sister speculates that this may have evoked chronic traumatic brain injury. Abusive head trauma according to the U.S. Centers for Disease Control and Prevention is an injury to the skull or intracranial contents of an infant or child younger than 5 years caused by inflicted blunt impact, violent shaking, or both. The constellation of findings may include injuries to the brain including the spinal cord. While I do not know exactly when Blanche started hitting me on the head, it may have started when I was ~7. A January, 2019 brain scan showed evidence of an old cortical lesion in my brain that could have been produced by her but the damage is too long past to draw such a conclusion.

In one incident with my sister when she was in junior high school, it was decided that she needed punishment for an infraction she does not remember. She had to go down in the basement, take off her clothes except for her under ware and kneel on the floor holding a chair. Blanche viciously whipped her, not stopping, while Betsy screamed and cried and saying that she was sorry. When Blanche was finished, my sister ran up to her room and looked in the mirror. She was cut, bloodied, bruised and black and blue all over her back and buttocks. She bled through her pajamas. The next day in gym class she had to change into gym clothes by trying to shield her injuries with her back to the wall so no one would see the wounds. It is an interesting fact that events coupled with severe pain and stress are remembered with great fidelity and often for a lifetime contributing to various forms of psychopathology.

There was a time when Blanche made Stanley, the obedient soldier, beat my sister. Apparently he did not want to, so he only hit her 3 or 4 times but they were good and hard strikes. Furthermore, given their Fundamentalist belief system, they forbade my sister from marrying a Catholic man. Rather an ironic twist as Stanley was originally a

Catholic himself. When Betsy found her soon to be betrothed, he was, of course, a Catholic and my parents preferred to disown her. Thus, my sister walked out of the house with her driver's license, bank book and a little cash and after that there was minimal contact with a very rare telephone call. Of note is the fact that my sister would start shaking until the call was ended. Even telephone calls from Blanche were a matter of stress reactions. Child abuse produces an automatic (also termed autonomic) conditioned response.

Let us end with an incident that was both humorous and pathetic at the same time and showing that Blanche could at times behave like a petulant child. Blanche would get lunch on the table for the 5 of us after church services. One Sunday she made hot dogs; oh yummy. A chef she was not as we ate a lot of meat loaf and if I was still hungry Stanley would say, "give him more bread." What a guy! After we all sat down in the dining room waiting to eat, I said something that set her off and she smacked me on the head, but she was so angry that she took the plastic mustard container and slammed it on the dining room table and the mustard came shooting out all over me and the table! We couldn't help laughing, including Dad. Well, then she got even more peeved so she stormed into her bedroom and slammed the door shut. We all chuckled for a bit more and then Dad said we needed to get a grip and clean up the mess. My sister reports that maybe she likes this memory because it was about "one for the good guys getting the upper hand."

There were other times in which the family had joint activities such as Blanche enjoying going with us all to visit her parents and other relatives in the Pennsylvania Dutch country. I would help my cousins carry the slop buckets for the pigs, milk the cows and watch while a chicken was beheaded and ran around headless for five minutes before succumbing to its wound.

Summary and suggestions. I present *extreme* forms of all religions as emotionally if not physically abusive. For the Christian Fundamentalists the claim that Jesus can replace emotional, human interactions is simply absurd; although it can be justified from the Bible. What does Jesus mean from a personal emotional perspective to a child even when provided with cute stories in colorful books about him in Sunday school? These images provide nothing of emotional content or a way to engage with their parents to resolve issues that could eventually produce psychopathology. The view that we should "be in but not of society" is equally absurd as practiced by Fundamentalists such as at BJU in South Carolina and Mormons in Utah (see for example, Tara Westover's book "Educated", Random House, 2018), and other sects. Praying is a means of considering personal issues inside one's own brain rather than a mode of external communication for resolution of emotional problems.

Besides breaking the bonds of *strict* religion, one must consider environmental (abusive) and genetic factors that are the actual causes of violence and aggression in society as a whole and more importantly in the family. Such issues cannot be completely resolved as abuse vulnerable individuals can suffer for a lifetime while we wait for biological treatments for such disorders that may take decades to develop. Survivors of abuse need the same empathy that cancer patients require even though the source of their suffering is hidden in their brains. Most importantly, it is not to be expected that such survivors will ever become normal socially or cognitively. I often hear the refrain, why do you not follow along in normal behaviors? It is because I am fundamentally sick even to this day.

The ADHD and Abuse-Damaged Brain

VIGNETTE
8

The First Beating: My ADHD Made Me Do It!

MY ADHD GENERATED some odd behaviors that my parents thought required severe punishment. Indeed, as noted above, it comes with symptoms such as impaired impulse control, delayed cognitive development and hyperactivity. As also noted, severe physical abuse is being hit with an object, burning, or penetrative sex for at least once a month for at least a year with very negative outcomes. My parents considered a life of Biblical obedience the key to resolving unregulated behaviors. However, extreme religious beliefs themselves can be a form of mental/emotional abuse. In our family it was the extreme of Christian Fundamentalism. The Catholic priest scandal is another form of religious abuse that was inevitable given their doctrine of celibacy for its priests. Pope Francis said, "it is as important an issue as the Reformation." However, they still refuse to remove the vow of celibacy which contradicts an essential law of biology; procreation for preservation of the species. That is a built-in human requirement.

When about 6, I was given a mixed breed dog that was all black except for his white paws, a white tip on his tail and snout and a white mark on his chest; hence his name Tippy. I mention him because Stanley was careful to explain that you should never hit a dog with your hand as he will become confused with your hand as a source of affection and discipline. Instead you should use a paper to hit them when training. Importantly, this appears to summarize his views on child rearing when

The First Beating: My ADHD Made Me Do It!

The Rutherford Reporter
May 5, 1955

Vandals identified. Mary Condomer reports
Police blotter; #4,678

Mr. James P. Putty, janitor at the Rutherford Elementary School reported that two second grade boys had a contest in the boys lavatory this afternoon to see who could urinate the highest on the wall. Although the wall was tiled, apparently Mr. Putty found washing it down to be out of his job description and reported the transgression to Principal Belcher. Police Chief "Irish" McGreggor said, "Criminals come in all shapes and sizes. These little f#@%ers were seen throwing snowballs at cars last winter. It is great that we finally have them in custody."

Ms. Belcher, a rotund woman in her late 50's, called the parents of each boy as Mr. Putty saw them leaving the site of their crime.

Brent "Red" Vogt

One of the boys was Brent "Red" Vogt, born in Manhattan in 1947 when his papa got home from combat in the Pacific. Mrs. Blanche E. Vogt was notified of the excremental effusion and found it quite horrifying. Imagine, her son peeing on a tiled wall in the lavatory. Who had ever heard of such a thing much less in a contest where the boys saw each other's outstretched winkies?

Mrs. Blanche Vogt assured Ms. Belcher that something would be done and she would take care of it like any responsible Christian parent. Thus, when hubby Stanley arrived home that evening from AT&T, he was presented with the facts of his son's incursion in the Elementary School lavatory. For the first time they had to confront a serious lack of moral fortitude in their son. And a Christian boy at that!

Bad boy "Red" was in his second floor bedroom where he could hear Blanche and Stanley deciding how to proceed. It was determined that their bad boy would lie upside-down and naked on his bed while Stan removed his leather belt looking at those little white buttocks. All the while Brent begged him not to beat him. Stan would have none of it as Blanche gave the orders in this house and he was a good soldier.

The beating went on until his white buttocks were red with blood and stained the sheets. Stan said, as he would many times in the future in between each carefully placed lash, "I am doing this for your own good, son."

When Condomer heard the form of discipline in the Vogt house, she said, "Hmmm, really? These Christian Fundamentalists don't apparently know how to discipline a child." The teachings of Christ were implemented by not sparing the rod; or leather belt as the case may be but how much blood needs to be shed?

Brother Brent was added to the prayer list of the Grace Episcopal Church so that his soul could be bathed in the redemptive blood of Jesus Christ. (There must be an irony somewhere in this approach to child abuse.)

Who won the excremental contest was never disclosed. Mr. Putty died 8 months later; "Red" ascribed his death to tattling on him. A tradition of harsh physical abuse ensued over the next 8 years. Many years of praying at Grace Church for Brent still does not seem to have taken hold of Christ's redemption. Join the parishioners in continuing to pray that Jesus will cure Brent's obvious psychopathologies. Prayer meeting will be held at 8:00 PM Wednesday followed by snacks and a fruity red wine to remind us of the blood that Christ shed on the cross.

Postsript

63

The absurdity of this disciplinary strategy was never apparent to my parents as they beat their children until they bled while never achieving the desired outcome. Should they have been using newspapers like with dogs? Thus, the religious approach in my family was to attempt to beat behaviors out of me and Betsy by not sparing the hand or leather belt.

Suggestions. It should be obvious, given the consequences of child abuse, that a parent should not beat, rape, neglect, or emotionally abuse their children as it will cause permanent brain damage and many possible adult chronic diseases as enumerated previously. Unfortunately, this is not obvious for many parents as noted by the percentage of parents that engage in corporal punishment and various other forms of abuse. Simply neglecting them is a form of abuse and must be stopped. Some parents may engage in emotional abuse and do not recognize the long-term consequences of their behavior for their children. This was certainly true for me.

VIGNETTE
9

The Coronet: An Evangelical Instrument and Severe Stress

ONE OF STANLEY'S joys was the trumpet. He likely enjoyed the blues, jazz and other classes of music in which the trumpet was often prominently featured that he may have heard in the Bronx and during his tour of duty in the Pacific during World War II. As with all of his joys, however, they were muted in relation to Blanche's more robust approach to religion and keeping him in his religious box. For example, his joys of epic movies such as *Ben Hur* was an equally sublimated desire as the ironic Fundamentalist view did not allow for the pleasures of watching movies including the great Biblical classics; a movie he noted he would love to take me too, but could not.

In order for Stanley to fulfill one of his dreams, he bought me a coronet which has a more mellow tone than the blare of a trumpet. I was given private lessons by a music instructor at Phillip's Academy in Andover, MA. I practiced in the basement for 30 minutes a day, 5 days a week. The teacher saw a spark of talent in my playing and wanted to teach me a full range of music beyond scales and hymns. Blanche went to the Academy and argued over playing the blues and jazz that she considered "worldly" and "inappropriate for a Christian boy" to play. She gave him the strict script to teach scales that would be used to play hymns to the glory of god. Needless to say, the instructor was not pleased but he did what he was told.

Stanley combined a number of his dreams with me in the form of his preaching and my playing the coronet. He did this by preaching in a park of Passaic, NJ, while holding his open Bible, to anyone who would stop and listen. I provided the musical interludes with my coronet. We also visited jails to preach and play for large groups of inmates; sometimes as many as 300. This was a good way for the inmates to get out of their cells and provide variation in an otherwise relatively boring routine. When I made a mistake, the inmates would burst out laughing causing a bit of embarrassment on my part but not too much as I had pity/empathy for their state. There are many religious conversions in jail as this was a way to get sympathy from the parole boards. We never knew how many "conversions" resulted ftom our Evangelical efforts.

You must wonder by now, why my playing the coronet is of any consequence much less of severe stress? Surely the inmate's laughter was not excessive and I had empathy for my "brothers" in jail. Was I really committed to playing the coronet for the deity's good graces? Is this but some pointless event that need not be considered further? More importantly, how does it relate to me and you? Actually, this is the beginning of the story in which the coronet becomes an instrument of intimidation, control and stress. Here the coronet is a symbol of any substantial and frequent (1-3 times per month) stressor. After reading this vignette one can substitute a different form of frequent stressor and consider its outcomes.

I was volunteered by my heartless mother to play at the front of the church before many services. I was extremely nervous and made so many mistakes that I was highly embarrassed and blushed profusely. This was obvious to all in the congregation and could not have gone unnoticed by even Blanche, but every few weeks her lack of compassion and empathy resulted in her making me go through this exercise over and over again. Given that she was a cold and distant woman, she had no feelings for what she was putting her son through. Indeed, this constant stress alone likely influenced an anxiety disorder that follows me to this day. When I refer to the coronet, it refers to a constant level of stress; one that is closely associated with religious experience. I suspect that many if not most of the parishioners had the relevant empathy for me and were sorry to see me put through such torment.

The advice of a cold mother was to pray about whatever emotional problems one experiences, as god will provide. In other words, I have nothing to offer you; let's see what Jesus has to say. This raises the question, Can Jesus replace human interactions and what does Jesus mean from a personal emotional perspective? If you are a "true" believer, there may be some solace in praying to this mythical figure. Like a placebo effect or hypnosis you may be able to induce a state in which you feel better after prayer. But for a growing number of people that are rejecting religious experience, this does not suffice for the affection and assistance that can be provided by thoughtful parenting.

Suggestions. Of course, the coronet is symbolic of any chronic stressor such as the fear of being bullied at school or anxiety over test taking. The reader only needs to fill in the blank that reflects upon their or their companions lives. Furthermore, one does not have to be an atheist to recognize that praying to a cold and distant deity does not replace the quality of emotionally close parenting and many religious parents understand this. Parental skills result from a close, caring, stable and protective family environment particularly during adolescence and pain and stress reduction are necessary features of familial interactions. I lived in a divided family and its outcroppings became apparent in me when I was raising my own family. A significant problem was the lack of empathy and emotional engagement; a form of abuse that I was not even aware of as an adult. Finally, remember that some individuals are vulnerable to stress and others are resilient. I was clearly the former. If you are vulnerable, you need to recognize this and realize that many of your internal struggles will not resolve and may be with you into adulthood. Anxiety drugs such as citalopram and clonazepam have value for me and I have directed my life to trying to resolve these problems in other survivors through my neuroscience research. The artists noted earlier also seek to help others but in different ways. Beth Hart, for example, has a neglectful father that appears to torment her to this day and influences her vocal efforts.

VIGNETTE **10**

Stanley: The Obedient Soldier and Further Beatings

STANLEY WAS LESS temperamental than Blanche. He learned how to take orders in the Army which he entered when 17. I was not very close to him but my favorite memory is of the times we went to the Andover town dump together on Saturday mornings once a month. In the dump I would scavenge for interesting items that others had thrown away. This was not, however, a time of intimate father-son relating but rather he did his thing and I did mine. He could have approached even this experience in a different manner but was devoid of how to best relate to his son.

My ADHD acted up many times, and the resulting behaviors drew scorn and anger from Blanche. As already noted before my first beating, she would tell me that when your father gets home you are going to be punished. As I knew what that meant, I would run up to my room where I could later hear mumbling between both parents on the first floor, while she made the case for punishment which often meant a beating. Again, the obedient soldier would walk up the stairs and I would start screaming, "no daddy please daddy don't beat me." As he takes his leather belt off and orders me to remove my cloths and lay on the bed upside down; "no daddy please daddy don't." Again, as the first lashes fell, he would say, "I am not doing this for myself, I am doing it for you." More lashes fell, "no daddy please daddy stop." The bleeding starts, "no daddy please daddy, no daddy please stop."

Maybe if the first beating was the last, they would have had a limited impact in my life and brain, but they did not stop. On one occasion while on my uncle's farm in Pennsylvania and working with my cousins on the combine bailing hay, I don't remember what I did wrong, I got yet another beating. This was done in someone else's home upstairs in the attic. My parents apparently had no shame in their violent mode of disciplining their children. What they were doing is conditioning my stress responses as discussed in Vignette 29.

When I was 16 and standing in the kitchen in Andover, Stanley was preparing for another "disciplinary action." At this point I was taller than him and had developed a mean and angry streak ironically thanks to his influence. I told him, "if you touch me one more time, I would beat the living shit out of you." The beatings stopped! Stanley appears to have recognized that he had met his match and he was too much of a coward to engage in further beatings or a fight at this time. He might now have to use methods that more closely approximated how other parents disciplined their children. However, I am certain he had no idea of what they were; i.e., nonviolent and nonabusive approaches.

Male aggression. Stanley's violence and aggression may have been evoked partially by his genetic makeup as I think was true for Blanche. However, it is also likely that his disorganized family upbringing until he entered the armed services at 17 could have been an important part of his problems. He was raised in the tenements of the Bronx along with other immigrant families. As already noted, he had 11 siblings that his mother could not adequately raise and he was "farmed out" to another family for rearing. His father was an alcoholic that died at age 55. These circumstances could provide him with no adequate model of paternal guidance. Indeed, the poverty of the family's low socioeconomic environment itself was likely a source of confusion and violence. Later we will consider the Cycle of Violence that he likely had been a part of. Taken in its totality, there were many factors that went into his willingness to beat his children; for our own good, of course.

A scientific perspective: Mouse genetics of aggression. It is a surprising fact that there is a mouse substrain that is exceedingly aggressive. The relevant genes likely have survival benefit in the wild so I would not try to pick one up as it will evoke vicious biting. Velez and colleagues (2010; *Behavioral Genetics*, volume 40, issue 2, pages 201–210l) found that males of this substrain behave consistently more aggressively toward a resident intruder with shorter attack times, more frequent attacks, and anti-social biting than healthy control mice. In addition, *isolation for a month dramatically increased this behavior.* Similar studies are needed for females and it should be noted that social isolation was a part of my religious upbringing and may have contributed to our parents and my aggression. Also, I am working with Sabrina van Heukelum and colleagues in the Netherlands to understand the reasons for this strain's behavior. Interestingly, neuron degenerative changes in cingulate cortex may, to some extent, mirror those observed in humans with conduct disorder. It is possible that a number of genes were responsible for some or much of my parent's aggression in addition to Stanley's upbringing in the Bronx.

Observations. Unfortunately, the slowly maturing brain of the adolescent does not allow them to immediately become aware of abusive situations, even when it is horrific maltreatment. This is why abuse can take one or more decades for survivors to recognize their maltreatment and come forward to authorities. It was not until I was 16 years old that I was able to recognize and stop it. I finally had the physical size, strength and anger to overpower Stanley. For others it can take much longer; either because of the level of abuse, their vulnerability or the physical weakness of the survivor to stop it such as during female rape.

VIGNETTE *11*

Child Abuse Reporting & Penalties

WHILE I AM not certain that my parents would have been caught abusing their children, thankfully times have changed as legal and social service organizations recognize the potential for serious long-term consequences to the psychiatric and physical health of survivors and mandatory rules have been put in place to protect these children and adolescents. If a physical education teacher had observed my sister's wounds in the account above, they would have been required to report it to social services. At that time, however, her only resort was to leave the family. Here we consider quotes from Mandatory Reporting Laws to protect children and adolescents.

Mandatory Reporting Laws: Child Abuse and Neglect
by Michael Spanow Law, Syracuse, NY
and FindLaw's legal writers and editors

"Incidences of child abuse and neglect have a profound effect on the lives of many children across the United States. Therefore, all states have set in place variations of mandatory reporting laws in order to decrease and prevent these incidents from occurring. These laws help ensure that cases of child abuse are reported to the authorities.

Mandatory reporting laws differ for each state when it comes to child abuse – which includes physical abuse, sexual abuse, and emotional abuse. However, it's important to remember that many of these laws also cover child neglect. In some states, these laws require that people in certain professions report child abuse and neglect to a proper authority, such as a law enforcement agency or child protective services. In other states, the mandatory reporting laws require *any* person who suspects child abuse or neglect report such instance.

According to information provided to the U.S. Department of Health and Human Services (HHS), there are 48 states that have mandatory reporting laws requiring certain people to report child abuse and neglect. These individuals are usually people who have frequent contact with children because of their occupation. The following is a sampling of mandatory reporters in the largest states:

California: teachers, teacher's aides, employees of day camps and youth centers, social workers, physicians, and clergy.

New York: physicians, dentists, licensed therapists, school officials, peace officers, and district attorneys.

Texas: any professionals who are licensed by the state or are employees of facilities licensed by the state and have direct contact with children, like teachers, nurses, doctors and juvenile probation officers.

Many other states have institutional reporting laws. These laws refer to individuals who work or volunteer for mandated reporters and who during their time of employment, gain knowledge of anything that may lead him or her to suspect abuse. In these situations, some states require that the staff member alert the head of the institution when he or she believes that an appropriate agency should be notified. Similarly, many states do not differentiate between professionals or institutions and require that anyone who has a suspicion of child abuse or neglect must report it.

Situations in which mandatory reporters must report vary

depending on state. However, according to the HHS, there are typically two standards as to when a report should be made:

When the reporter has reason to believe or suspects that a child has been abused or neglected.

When the reporter sees a child being subjected to harm or knows of conditions that would reasonably result in harm to the child.

Failure to comply with the mandatory reporting requirements can not only result in criminal penalties, but they can also subject a child to continued abuse or neglect. If you have questions about the mandatory reporting laws in your state, it's in your best interest to speak with an experienced criminal defense attorney near you."

Finally, in the instance of rape, in a timely manner, reporting and documentation is of great importance. I will not go into the details here but suggest that the reader watch *Grey's Anatomy,* Season 15, Episode 19. While our parents were not sexual predators, they clearly engaged in child abuse, and if reported, would have been subject to legal charges. There are penalties for child abuse as considered by the above quoted group and continued here.

"In most states, child abuse may be charged as either a felony or a less serious offense, depending on the circumstances. The most severe cases can carry harsh child abuse sentences, including felony lifetime sentences, while the least serious cases are considered gross misdemeanors which could potentially result in no prison time. Punishment will typically be more severe if the offender has a prior record of criminal child abuse activity and greatly reduced if there is no prior record.

For sentencing purposes, a person charged with child abuse may enter a plea of guilty, not guilty, or no contest. In many cases, sentencing can include probation or a prison term of up to five years. Sentencing in more serious cases may include a longer prison term. Other possible penalties and/or consequences can include: Termination of parental rights, ruined reputation, criminal record, supervised access to the child, physical or actual loss and enjoyment of a child, continual involvement with a child protective services agency."

These are the possible outcomes for my parents in today's environment where child abuse is not tolerated and must be reported. If caught after the first beating, these types of charges would have limited my abuse and had a much less severe impact on my life and brain. But then, there are other forms of abuse they were not aware of and would not have stopped even if they were aware of them given their Biblical views.

VIGNETTE **12**

Strong Links Between Maltreatment and PTSD

ONE COMMON CONSEQUENCE of maltreatment is PTSD as they share many epidemiological (population demographics), symptoms, causes and predictive outcomes. The second picture in Vignette 1 shows this link. While in my experience, playing the coronet in front of a large church congregation likely contributed to my PTSD, it was also influenced by severe abuse. There are four primary symptoms of PTSD including; 1) re-experiencing the event(s) via nightmares, flashbacks and/or intrusive recollections, 2) avoiding reminders associated with the event(s), 3) negative mood and thinking, and 4) excess arousal of heart rate and breathing particularly under stress conditions. My church and abuse experiences were, and likely still are, responsible for evoking PTSD symptoms even as an adult. It is also the case that child-abuse related PTSD is the most severe form of PTSD.

Drug responses provide evidence for some conclusions about my various disorders because these responses have predictive value; i.e., if the drug does not have efficacy, it is less likely that I have/had a particular disorder. I am taking Zoloft (Sertraline) which is a selective serotonin (a neurotransmitter used by neurons for communication) uptake blocker that increases serotonin in the brain including particularly sACC. It has efficacy for PTSD and for me thus supporting the view that I had child-abuse related PTSD that plagues me to this day. Many of the following statements and viewpoints I derived from my own experiences and those of Kearney and colleagues (2010; *Clinical Child and Family Psychological Reviews,* volume 13, pages 46-76) and supporting references (~350) are in this article.

Children faced with abusive parents are at risk for poor regulation of the pituitary gland and its chemical secretions (see Emily's brain in Vignette 2 for where it is located). Secure attachment status, appropriate social/parental feedback, and responsible and sensitive parental care are especially important influences on development of what is called the pituitary axis. Alterations in this developmental trajectory produce impairments that continue among adults with a history of childhood maltreatment. Children with pituitary dysregulation act aggressively and otherwise inappropriately, leading to maladaptive disciplinary practices. This suggests that my maltreatment itself may have caused some of the behaviors for which I was subsequently beaten, not just my ADHD-related behaviors.

In contrast, some children and adolescents may be *buffered* from the major biological effects following maltreatment by certain genetic characteristics, good affect regulation and cognitive functioning, positive self-concept, social support, proximity to a non-offending and caring parent, cultural factors, key learning experiences, or even extended dissociation from such events. In other words, resilient individuals may have factors that help them to avoid the worst outcomes experienced by vulnerable patients. Many of these I did not have such as good cognitive functioning (ADHD), social support from my parents, and proximity to a non-offending parent as both engaged in my abuse. As I am a vulnerable individual without these supports, particularly in terms of my parents, I was not "buffered" from their abuse.

Chronically maltreated youths have great difficulty understanding their environment and may not develop or execute appropriate methods for coping with stress or solving problems. Problems in emotional and behavioral self-regulation can then lead to excessive anxiety, depression, cognitive distortions, somatization, dissociation from such experiences, aggression, impulsivity, suspiciousness, and other systemic maladaptive responses all of which can be associated with ADHD as well. Common long-term effects of maltreatment include school failure and absenteeism, less anticipation of attending college, social and thought problems, physical and sexual revictimization, violence perpetration, and various psychopathologies such as depression, substance abuse, personality disorders, PTSD and other anxiety disorders in adulthood. Maltreatment was a particularly salient trauma for PTSD in my adolescence because it involved physical violence, injury, and coercion. Maltreatment can also lead to ancillary traumas such as separation from family members; indeed, my parents encouraged my separation from my brother to sterilize his environment from my influence and my sister was disowned for marrying a Catholic man.

PTSD is especially likely in maltreatment cases involving physical abuse with longer duration of maltreatment, threat or force, feelings of guilt, exaggerated startle responses, and a perception that one has been victimized. PTSD in maltreated youths is associated with many types of behavior problems. Prominent examples include somatic complaints, social withdrawal, fear, depression, social and cognitive problems, poor school performance and social competence, and delinquent and aggressive behaviors. These comments stand for children and adolescents that have been raped as well, but that was not my particular issue.

Maltreated boys with symptoms of PTSD are at risk of using threatening behaviors or physical abuse against dating partners. Youths with PTSD demonstrate a stronger relationship between exposure to parental violence and interpersonal aggression toward friends or romantic partners than youths without PTSD. I once punched a girlfriend after a date so hard that she fell to the floor. The image of her on the floor will never leave my brain. We were both stunned and I did not know then, but do now, that this was an expression of my adolescent abuse. Also, one is more prone to violent actions with PTSD. As an angry young man on the Orange Line subway in Boston, I intervened in a fight between a man and a woman; in this instance to protect her rather than hurt her. No matter how hard I punched this man, he would not stay down, likely because he was high on drugs. Most people would not have intervened but I had no such trepidations nor would I today as my ADHD and PTSD live on in my brain.

The severity, duration, frequency, unpredictability, and proximity of threatening, harmful, and uncontrollable stressors are important risk factors for the eventual development of PTSD. Trauma may involve a single event or, in many maltreatment cases, repeated events that may become predictable over time as in my case due to continued activation of the stress response to church playing of the coronet and frequent abuse.

Cognitive vulnerabilities as already noted for ADHD are also expressed for patients with PTSD. Their inability to sufficiently process traumatic events leads to impaired emotionality, disruptions of previously held and potentially rigid views about safety of self and the world, perpetuated beliefs about ongoing threat, impaired habituation of symptoms from ongoing avoidance of trauma-based thoughts, negative self-evaluation regarding competence, and self-blame regarding traumatic events. These problems are maintained by poor verbal processing of the events, intense emotions such as anger, maladaptive appraisals of life events and future harm, negative appraisals about one's vulnerability and recovery immediately after trauma. Internal causal attributions of negative events, attentional bias toward threat, thought suppression and avoidance, rumination, excessive worry, and distraction are also problematic. My negative views of the world were particularly evident during my transition period in the form of art when I had no parental or other support systems to assist me in coping.

The above issues in adolescents can become generalized as patients may fear other, related situations. Operant conditioning may then occur when a youth actively avoids thoughts, situations, or reminders of the trauma to reduce fear and anxiety. The fear response thus fails to extinguish memories of the trauma and PTSD symptoms are maintained. Powerful emotional responses in addition to fear that can pervade these learning processes include horror and helplessness. The role of learning in maltreated individuals is considered in Vignette 29.

There are treatment interventions and I believe the late Dr. Marco Alfondary, who I will formally introduce you to below as he appears later in my Lifeline, was shrewd in how he guided me away from my negative self-viewpoints and relationships to more healthy approaches. We never discussed the conceptual framework of psychotherapy but rather he dug in with me into the meat of my personal issues. I miss him to this day. Primary interventions in this regard and for PTSD in particular include debriefing and cognitive-behavioral and relaxation therapy, art, play, and pharmacological therapies such as Zoloft as already noted. Indeed, the role of art for some performers has been noted. More specific approaches include psychoeducation, hypnotherapy, grief work, affect regulation, interpersonal skills development, narrative story-telling, coping skills, stress inoculation training, and exposure-based practices, either individually or in a group format. Cognitive-behavioral approaches demonstrate the best efficacy and a key first step to any of these therapies is to develop a close therapeutic alliance with the therapist to help patients express feelings of helplessness, shame, and vulnerability and identify the meanings of traumatic events and symptoms of PTSD. I refer again to Marco as these techniques depend on a strong therapeutic relationship to reduce embarrassment, focus on cathartic release of anger, relieve guilt and shame, and develop a more positive self-image.

A critical proviso for expectations of stress relief is that brain changes occur that may impede progress. We know from experimental animal studies that stress prunes dendrites in cingulate cortex. If this is true in the human brain, it will interfere with neuron-to-neuron communication as the dendrites are critical sites of inputs from other neurons. On a grander scale this would be expected to interfere with cognitive, emotional and social behaviors in the limbic system.

Conclusions and Suggestions. As I have lived my entire life with ADHD and the cascade of negative, maltreatment events leading to PTSD, it is difficult to identify when the cognitive and emotional problems of ADHD leave off and when those of maltreatment begin. They are too intertwined in the circuitry of my brain to disentangle, although my responses to Zoloft are informative. The concept of "buffering" as encountered by resilient individuals is important to recognize because this buffering provides insights into how to treat children and adolescents to avoid the most pernicious outcomes of abuse and even possibly ADHD. As I am not a psychotherapist, I can only hope that readers with issues similar to mine can find their Marco as early as possible; he is a symbol of successful therapeutic intervention. We are about to consider how relaxation in the Andover basement and town forest was so important to me; escape hatches as an accidental form of relaxation therapy not planned or organized by a therapist. My drawing was also an accidental form of therapy from my anger, internalized depressive symptoms and a very negative view of myself and the world. Finally, while I have not considered rape, remember that it is a form of physical abuse and many of the issues raised in this vignette relate to these experiences as well. The adolescent girls and boys that have been repeatedly raped also need to find their Marco.

VIGNETTE *13*

Refuge in the Basement

I HAVE ALWAYS known that school did not click for me during the first years in Rutherford, NJ or the early years in middle school in Andover, MA. In the latter, school class interruptions were still numerous. For example, there was a project in which a group was going to send a weather balloon to collect data high up in the atmosphere. I was so disruptive that the teacher had to take me out of the exercise. This, of course, is another example of how my ADHD symptoms interfered with my early school work including my science education.

Late in the eighth grade a science teacher lent me a biology book and it was pure magic to me. As I was completely engaged reading it, I started going to the town library to read the *Scientific American* and other books and journals. Suggested projects at the end of the *Scientific American* led me to start thinking of doing my own projects. I also learned deep respect for librarians who helped me find information to support these activities. One of my great joys in graduate school at Boston University School of Medicine was walking down Longwood Avenue to Harvard's Countway Medical Library. In their basement are the very oldest collection of journals and books, some of which were relevant to my studies of the medial surface of the brain such as C. and O. Vogt (1919; Allegemeine Ergebnisse unserer Hirnforschung. *Journal for Psychology and Neurology,* volume 25, pages 279-462). Don't worry, I cannot remember my undergraduate German either. The smell itself in the stacks was pungent and I remember it to this day.

Unfortunately, I have not seen a librarian in the last two decades as the internet and Google have all but replaced them.

Mr. Aristotle Virgaropolous, a short Greek, biology teacher, took us through the woods around the high school in Andover where we collected leaves in the fall and preserved them for making tracings of their veins. His fervor for biology was obvious and it spilled into my consciousness as I would never lose my love of biology or his face for that matter. We dissected frogs and I would chase the girls with my dissections acting out my ADHD symptoms in just another way. I enjoyed chemistry but simply could not understand "Leo the Lion Goes Ger"; loss of electrons is oxidation, while gain of electrons is reduction. As I had never seen an electron, this was difficult for me to understand no matter how much Mr. Danforth tried to explain it to me.

There was a turning point early in high school when I submitted a project to the science fair. Surprisingly, I actually won a prize for my work in bacteriology. I will never forget the moment when Mr. Danforth looked in the back door of our chemistry class with a face full of amazement, one could say shock, and signaled for me to come out of the room. Here he had a student that was clearly struggling with the course material but could produce an outstanding science project. He was incredulous to say the least. The project went on to the Massachusetts Institute of Technology state science fair and won an honorable mention. After that he worked harder with me and I received a "B" in chemistry; likely more for my effort and project than test taking abilities. Although my cognitive abilities were still lagging, this was the beginning of my scientific career; one built on experimentation rather than book learning. Learning how to test hypotheses rather than using belief systems like those codified in religious texts.

Another benefit of succeeding in science fairs was that I had unrestricted access to the chemistry stock room which provided me with many compounds for making bombs and other activities as well as developing projects. I remember Mr. Danforth correcting papers at his desk one day and not even looking up as I went in and out of the storage room to collect my harvest of chemicals. Many young boys go through a bomb-making period and blowing up very large blocks of concrete was great fun. My later science fair projects included "Oxygen-Carbon Dioxide Balance in Life" for which I received an honorable mention and one titled "Chromatography Absorption Analysis." In this latter project I crushed leaves, dissolved the mixture in acetone and placed it on filter paper. It turns out that there are multiple proteins in leaves with different colors that could be detected as they migrated through the filter paper and this was one of the first paper chromatography studies ever performed. For this I went to the MIT state fair again and won High Honors. The school newspaper referred

Refuge in the Basement

to me as "a professional science fair winner." The above picture is of my basement lab next to the oil storage tank.

In a family where religious violence, be it emotional or physical, was a norm, I retreated to the cool, quiet basement where the only indication of a parent was the laundry. I did not recognize it at the time, but do now, that this was a form of relaxation therapy. All of my personal activities were conducted there in my escape refuge rather than in my bedroom in the attic where I was disciplined. The basement is where I learned my love of reading books assigned for the summer months of high school; Moby Dick, Tom Sawyer, Captains Courageous, Mutiny on the Bounty, Nancy Drew Mysteries and many others. I practiced my coronet there for one-half hour a day for 5 days a week; mostly boring scales. There also was an open area where at one time I had a model train set that I made mountains and other natural features out of plaster of pares and planted moss to make bushes. On other occasions, I had a ping-pong table for playing with neighborhood friends. We got so good that we mostly played off the table using spinning and other techniques to confound our opponent as the ball would spin in different and unpredictable directions when it hit the table. Thus, all of my important activities went on in the basement.

The town forest also provided refuge where I had a small dug out log cabin. I often spent too much time exploring the forest on Sundays and when I returned late to leave for Sunday night services received the inevitable reprimand and spanking. On one occasion, I built a fire in the small fireplace and set the entire structure on fire. Fortunately for my buttocks, a hunter arrived and with his jacket helped me quell it. Sadly, the forest is gone now as it has been a victim of home development. Where will the ADHD and abused adolescents go to escape their family problems?

Conclusions. Sustaining life in a family rife with psychopathology requires a retreat and I found mine in the town forest and basement in Andover MA. These retreats were an accidental form of relaxation therapy and established a lifetime approach which was reinstated during the 2000s when much of my scientific work was done in a 2000 square foot, renovated cellar in Manlius, NY. Indeed, this book and our scientific opus *Cingulate Neurobiology and* Disease (2009, Oxford University Press, 853 pages) was written in this basement. Reading, art in all its forms, writing ("journaling") and science all can be used to cope with abusive environments and relaxation therapy should be considered by ADHD and abuse survivors along with various drug therapies.

VIGNETTE *14*

The Vogt Family as a Model of Poor Social Bonding

THE FAMILY IS a critical social unit that historically precedes religious and other forms of affiliating. It is meant to provide a stable environment for relations between two people, their children and their common goals in child rearing. Family members share bonds and generally maintain a common set of values. During my life, I was often asked why I had such a nonchalant view of family and why I did not make the family the top priority in my life. Why did I not focus on family issues when attempting suicide? The answer is that I was not raised in a normal and healthy family with such values. A good and well known example of the family as a predisposing priority is that of Joe Biden. Although his decision to not run for the presidency in 2016 was a complex one, his son Beau had died during the run up to the election and he said family matters were one of the reasons he would not run even though the presidency had been a life-long goal.

In my childhood family, our parents mistreated their first two children greatly disrupting the possibility for forming close relationships with them. I am certain they were not aware of its impact on family cohesion as their childhood families had looser bonding due in part to their extremely large families where bonding may not have been effective. This is particularly not surprising for Stanley who had poor family relationships in his context of 11 siblings in the Bronx. As noted earlier, he was "farmed out" to another family that could make a best effort to raise him. Like me, he had no model around which to formulate and guide family relationships. Blanche remains a question mark, although she was also from a large 11 children family and may have not acquired the tools with which a healthy family is maintained. Indeed, she made her best effort to pull the family apart.

Given my difficulties with ADHD and parental abuse, I was viewed as an outlier in the family; a black sheep if you would. My sister saw how I was abused and she was abused as well; this did not help her engage emotionally in our family setting. I was explicitly told by my parents to avoid my 9-year younger brother so I would not influence him in a negative way. Their will upon death explicitly did not mention passing anything to me; not that I needed it as I was long ago independent both emotionally and financially. Stanley, always the good soldier doing what he was told, made his resources available to the younger son to build a house for his family that was simply transferred to him upon his father's death. When given the option after his death to share the assets or cut communication permanently, Brian chose the latter and we never spoke again. One could say he was simply carrying out the wishes of his parents as the good son would be expected to do but I would say he was greedy as is true in many families where there is bickering over the family assets. Thus, it is noteworthy that even the good son had impaired priorities and views of family bonding.

In each child it is clear that my parents were unable to form a family unit with strong bonding among its individuals. Thus, given our parent's efforts to actively tear apart their family, it is not surprising that I came to raising a family without the tools to see and encourage strong family ties. I drew blanks when asked the above questions because I lacked a model of how a normal family interacts. I was not a perfect father, although I did not physically abuse my children as a matter of choice. However, family as a cohesive unit was not part of my world view or driver of my daily behavior. While I did not bury my head in the sand like religious zealots, I could not seem to visualize how a structured and happy family operates. For this I had to largely depend on my second wife and her family.

The triple-hit model for poor parenting. As noted earlier, an adolescent with ADHD has parental attachment issues as a matter of course. Unfortunately this problem was amplified for me and my sister by harsh physical, neglectful and emotional abuse that always kept me and her at a distance from our parents in what I term "the triple-hit model of parental abuse." They also were unable to love us and respond appropriately to our emotional needs. Giving us blank stares and telling us to talk with the Lord about our problems simply enhanced my detachment from them and impacted my future family life. This is the triple-hit model of abuse where the adolescent is abused at all possible levels. Indeed, I had no concept of family when marrying my first wife, neither did she, and the marriage blew up. Thus, different forms of abuse can build on each other in an additive manner to become even more deleterious to brain functioning and family bonding.

Summary and suggestions. Individuals that are vulnerable to serious life stresses (remember the vulnerable/resilient dichotomy) have difficulty forming natural family bonds. This is one of the messages for the life partners of vulnerable, child-abused survivors. A conscious effort is needed to establish appropriate family bonding practices likely in a family therapy context. Notably, my sister and I received such "training" from our in-laws as adopted families but I think my sister was more effective at and committed to such activities than I was.

VIGNETTE
15

Sex

MY FIRST KISS was from a girl in the Andover Middle School and was a sign of true affection. She snuck up behind me and kissed me briefly on the cheek. Unfortunately, the teacher observed this activity as she retreated to her desk. I stammered out a few sentences of explanation to him with my very, very red face suggesting that my words did not match the obvious facts. It was then that the teacher explained to me what a "red herring" was. Indians dragged dead fish across their path in the forest to throw off their scent to potential prey or predators. It is also something that misleads or distracts from a relevant or important question. He was having just too much fun tormenting me but I remember it with great fondness as an affectionate crush.

Here we move forward in my life to when I was 20 years old and beyond kissing. The subject of sex is the beginning of Christian efforts to downplay as much as possible the most important of animal behaviors; preservation of the species. The Biblical book of Genesis espouses the story of Adam and Eve being thrown out of the Garden of Eden for eating the apple; one assumes this refers to their getting it on in sexual congress. Now this is an odd paradox. God puts the urge to have sexual intercourse in Adam and Eve's brains but when they employ it, they are punished. The Catholic Church takes this issue to its extreme with priests and nuns not being allowed to engage in sex with a vow of celibacy. The irony of the Catholic priest scandal is that it is based on another form of religious abuse. As noted earlier, Pope Francis said that it is as important an issue as the Reformation! In 2019 Pope Francis issued the first law obligating officials in the Roman Catholic Church worldwide to report cases of clergy sexual abuse and attempts to cover it up to their superiors. The decree was Francis' response to address a crisis that devastated the church and clouded his legacy. "The crimes of sexual abuse offend Our Lord; cause physical, psychological and spiritual damage to the victims; and harm the community of the faithful." The difficulty here is that, once again, religious teaching attempts to replace the biological force of reproduction with unjustified belief systems. The strongest urge in any biological ecosystem is the effort of its members to reproduce. Thus, the effort to have priests and nuns live a life of celibacy is absurd.

In our family I was given no counselling or sex education. Even today, Blanche would have gone to school authorities to have me removed from sex education classes as she did when students were taught how to dance and socially affiliate. So my first experiences with sex were with men who took a liking to slender young adolescent males. While reading the Bible in my room for overflow student housing in the YMCA at the Philadelphia College of the Bible (boy, this group of religious zealots was really out of touch with reality by putting young male students in the YMCA), a gay man felt my genitals under the Bible as I tried to witness to him about the salvation he could receive from Jesus Christ. In another instance one picked me up at the bus station in New York City, took me to his room, showed me pictures of naked women and tried to have intercourse. It did not "work" of course as I had no clue about anal sex or any other sex for that matter. He concluded that I had been too "busy" the night before to perform with him. A nice thought, I guess, at least he was giving me a break.

I clearly remember sitting with Blanche and Stanley, in their bedroom, of all places, and telling them of these experiences. Neither one had any visible expression or insights to offer; not even any grand religious perspectives other than, as always, take the issue in prayer to the Lord. Unfortunately, that advice had no value to a 20 year-old boy as imaginary communication lines to Heaven apparently were not working for me. How could I imagine the Lord's advice if I did not understand the topic of discussion? This was not the first time I drew a blank in the activity of praying. It should also be noted that such an approach had no intimate, emotional connection for me. This too was an imaginary response of the supplicant. Without parental guidance, I was lost and cut off from the realities of everyday life in a form of neglect including guidance on matters of sex.

And then along came Helen! While working in financial analysis at Exxon (then Esso) in Linden, NJ as part of a cooperative education experience for a total of 9 months, I dated Helen. She was a cute and slender lady and we would engage in the normal dating activities of going out to eat and spent much time in the car talking. Surprisingly, I never "made a move" on her and this certainly was something of a surprise as the New Jersey girls were, shall we say, enlightened in the ways of sexual exploration. We did a bit of kissing but nothing further is all that I considered. Amazingly, I had not an inkling as to why we were dating, no urge to engage in fondling, no clue as to what other adolescents were doing when "parking," and no expectation that I would have a family some day. At one point I was worried that she might have gotten pregnant! In retrospect this was not even possible given the level of our activities together yet I thought it a miracle and brought her flowers to celebrate. This goes to show how totally uninformed I was on matters of sex. My parents had succeeded in completely isolating me from such realities. One of the few times Blanche stood up for me was when a cub scout den mother accused me of pinching her butt which Blanche knew was not possible.

Later in a semester, Helen came to Boston for a short visit to provide me with a lesson in sexual experience that she must have received from one of those more experienced New Jersey boys we hear so much about. She laid me down in my dorm room bed in a building on the Fenway in Boston, climbed into the saddle and rode me hard. I was, to say the least, totally amazed at such an activity. For the first time I was shown what no other woman had shown me and it was pure bliss. I had taken a bite of the proverbial apple and it was great.

No wonder we are all going to Hell. After sharing her newly found expertise in sexual intercourse, Helen went back to New Jersey never to be heard from again.

Conclusions. While Helen showed me the other invaluable use of my second brain, what was missing was the connection between sex and emotional engagement. My second wife actually learned about such relations in church and school, but once again, I had no such direction. Sex for me has always been independent of how I felt towards the few ladies that I dated and this produced a lack of insight into their experiences, goals, and the potential meaning of our relationships. This certainly had an impact on my selection and involvement with my first wife. Fortunately, things changed for the better with my second wife and "The Good Years" as noted on my Lifeline began. However, I first had to break the entanglements of strict Fundamentalist Christianity and get a grip on my psychiatric issues.

VIGNETTE *16*

Art Expresses Emotion and Internal Turmoil

CLASSICAL ARTISTS SUCH as Leonardo da Vinci, Rembrandt, Michelangelo, John William Waterhouse and William Blake painted landscapes, figures and portraits that were so close to reality that they look much like photographs. Indeed, their work was emotionally neutral. However, not all art seeks to replicate reality as a photograph. We have already considered Antwone Fisher's and Beth Hart's art and abuse struggles in Vignette 1. Here I would like to start with the life and painting of Edvard Munch before moving into my much more modest efforts. Most readers know of his work *"The Scream."* He was born in 1863 in what is now Oslo, Norway, to a military doctor. His childhood experiences with death and sickness, both his mother and sister died of tuberculosis, greatly influenced his emotional and intellectual development. This and his father's *fanatic Christianity* led Munch to view his life as dominated by the "twin black angels of insanity and disease." I have confirmed the negative impact that extreme Christian Fundamentalism can have on an adolescent's development. Edvard Munch said, "When I paint, I never think of selling. People simply fail to understand that we paint in order to experiment and to develop ourselves as we strive for greater heights." What he is saying is that the normal brain cannot understand the internal struggles of the artist.

Art Expresses Emotion and Internal Turmoil

"The Scream," painted in 1893, depicts Edvard's internal suffering and anxieties. Munch reports his feelings that drove creation of this work. *"I was walking along the road with two friends. The sun set. I felt a tinge of melancholy. Suddenly the sky became a bloody red. I stopped, leaned against the railing, dead tired. And I looked at the flaming clouds that hung like blood and a sword over the blue-black fjord and city. My friends walked on. I stood there, trembling with fright. And I felt a loud, unending scream piercing nature."*

Art in my life at age 21. I was long aware of the roll of emotion in pain processing in the brain even before entering graduate school. Long before the neuroscientific community recognized this amazingly obvious fact, I was aware that the key to understanding pain was its triggering of emotional responses in the limbic system. These facts appeared to me in my Transitional Period as I turned inward and expressed them in a number of ways artistically.

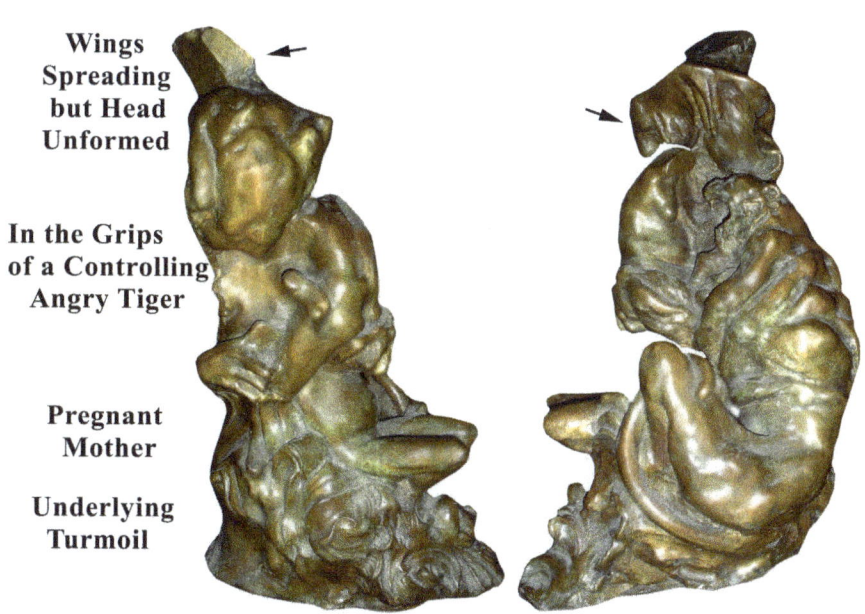

Wings Spreading but Head Unformed

In the Grips of a Controlling Angry Tiger

Pregnant Mother

Underlying Turmoil

To conceptualize my life to age 21, I decided to commission a bronze sculpture of my life that would depict its evolution from bottom

95

to top. A young lady of about my age with the last name Rubin, I do not remember her first name, listened to me describe what I wanted in the composition and followed it exactly as I described it to her. The above picture shows the front (left) and back (right) and labelling beginning at the bottom where stormy seas reflect the underlying turmoil encountered by me and my sister in the Vogt family. My pregnant mother is shown followed by my being held in the grips of an angry tiger with its left upper incisor tooth exposed as tigers do when threatened (right picture). This is a reflection of the cold religious upbringing I had and also reflects the fear of being engulfed by my parents and their religion as the ribs of the tiger are the fingers of a human hand holding me with crushing force. Surprisingly, two final touches at the top suggest hope. On the right there are wings suggesting that flight from my demonic parents and their strict religious beliefs could be achieved. Moreover, on the left my head is shown as an unformed block rather than as it was at the time. This is because I did not know where I would be going in life once freed from this violent family. I now know.

When the sculpture was finished, Miss Rubin's mother visited to see her work. The two of them conversed quietly in a corner of the room so I could not hear their dialogue. They both were hugging and crying. It has always been my thought that Miss Ruben had been abused at some point in her adolescence and that is why she was so adept at interpreting my wishes for the work and why they were upset when sharing the experience of my/her sculpture. I hope that it speaks to other abuse survivors who can add their own interpretations.

In Philadelphia, while attending the Philadelphia College of Bible, I spent much time in the Rodan museum with his sculpture of the *"Gates to Hell."* This was likely Stanley's view of Hell that he was "saving" me from by "not sparing the rod." He really took the scriptures as truth to beat the hell out of me. The sculpture is shown with an excellent photograph by Roman Suzuki via *Wikimedia Commons (CC BY 3.0).* While this sculpture was never finished, the Thinker is embedded in its top, possibly reflecting the human consideration of life choices and outcomes. Below and around its edges are Rodan's view of Hell and the torture of its members in eternal damnation. This reflects the view of my parents and the outcome Stanley was trying to "help" me avoid with harsh physical abuse; it being for my own good of course!

Between the ages of 21 and 22 I was in a particularly depressed state as indicated by my self-portrait at this time and other works. I went back to the Church of the Open Bible in Burlington, MA that I attended while living in Andover, played my coronet before services, and had choir practice. As I walked through the main sanctuary and basement where church functions and Sunday school were held, I felt an overwhelming fear of this environment and never returned to it again. I also avoided all interactions with the people I knew when growing up. Avoidance of fearful triggers is one symptom of posttraumatic stress disorder and this symptom and others continue in me to this day.

The face is an important reflection of the current emotional state of an individual and statements can be made with self-portraits that are not possible in any other way including written text. In my early 20s I was going through a transition from my life as a Fundamentalist Christian with a regimented perspective on values, life goals and success by depending on "the blood of Jesus Christ" to a secular life where I determined who I was rather than living as a vessel to be reflected by Jesus Christ. As I said at that time, "I am creating a new person who can become whatever internal and external realities dictate." Of course, the strict moral code and work ethic learned in my youth were relevant and not lost, but I was now in the driver's seat and not beholden to a religious leader through which the values of Jesus Christ and Biblical teachings were 2 millennia old.

Such a transition, as noted on my Lifeline at ages 20-24, is catastrophic, especially to an adolescent without adequate support systems, and my artistic work reflected that. Many adolescents with family and other abuse-relevant issues such as contemplating suicide, Borderline Personality Disorder (BPD) and PTSD turn to drugs for self-medication, I turned to art and neuroscience.

The ADHD and Abuse-Damaged Brain

This self-portrait shows a seriously angry and depressed youth with a drawn face in the context of turmoil and the statement "Dead Birds Fly." This statement reflects the fact that what you see is not reality. A bird flying usually signifies life and cheerfulness, but in my world view it was simply a delusion. I produced another piece in which the world is depicted in full pastel colors on the left but behind it on the right was a completely black and disheartening world with lightening indicating a storm. Again, what you see in everyday life is not reality.

Art Expresses Emotion and Internal Turmoil

Picasso said, "you must paint what you know is there, not what you see."

In another piece called "Hands" there are a number of things that stand out. One is self-mutilation with the knife and blood splashing and streaming from my arm. I never cut myself as adolescent girls with BPD often do to self-injure themselves, but this picture clearly shows an impulse to such a behavior. I was also suicidal at this time. The bars emphasize the jail of previous religious constraints and one of my hands grabbing a bar in an effort to exit this torment. A third hand reaches up and also reflects my desire to escape a life of mental torment and suffering. The fact that it is there at all may indicate a sense of hope; knowing that there were other possibilities.

These views appear occasionally in my dreams decades later. Our brains are quite active during sleep as they consolidate memories possibly to better use brain real estate. In one dream, for example, I was climbing a large staircase with some close colleagues and an early mentor. As we ascended there was general conversation and at the top of the stairs we opened a door to view the world. It was virtually flooded with water; the winds were howling in a tempest, there were a few trees above the water and occasional houses floated by in the water. This is not what one would expect when leaving a building except during a hurricane.

While on the subject of dreams, I must recount another rather provocative dream as they can recreate scenarios with stored emotional and cognitive information in the brain that reflect attitudes toward the present or past. In this particular dream I dragged Blanche down into the cellar where I spent most of my time. There I sat on the cold cement floor, turned her over in my lap and pulled her dress up to expose her buttocks. With my bare hand I beat her until she bled. I am certain that Freud would have greatly enjoyed hearing of this dream and trying to understand my life through this lens. It expressed my obvious hatred for Blanche.

Conclusions. Each of these works and dreams reflect a deep depression associated with a significant emotional and personal transition out of a life of abuse and religious control. Internalizing depression and anxiety are consequences of harsh adolescent abuse. Many survivors employ various art forms to express their internal strife, fears, and anxieties as noted in this vignette and the first one. Alan Cumming asked an excellent question, "what would I be doing if not for this career that provides me with the adrenaline surge I need in my life?" I suggest that he might have engaged in aggression and violence as part of the Cycle of Violence. The conjunction of artistic expression as psychotherapy; be it professional or simply for personal benefit, is an important avenue to dealing with the survivor's internal struggles.

VIGNETTE
17

Jesus Christ Superstar

WE ARE NOW **moving along in my Lifeline during the transitional years. I worked during many summer vacations at Dave Lundquist's greenhouses in Woburn, MA and during some vacations from undergraduate school. "Lunk," as he was often called, was surprised at my interest in the rock opera** *"Jesus Christ Superstar."* I have recounted above the many ways that religious fundamentalism impacted my life and, of course, these were not Lunk's experiences nor did he know of mine. In fact he led the young people's organization for kids up to about 18-years old including me.

"Jesus Christ Superstar" is a 1970 rock opera with music by Andrew Lloyd Webber and lyrics by Tim Rice. I still have the Playbill from attending it in 1971 when it played in the Mark Hellinger Theatre in New York City. The musical started as a rock opera album before its Broadway debut and it is mostly sung with little spoken dialogue. The story is loosely based on the Gospels' accounts of the last week of Jesus's life, beginning with the preparation for his arrival and his disciples in Jerusalem and ending with the crucifixion. It depicts political and interpersonal struggles between Judas Iscariot and Jesus that are not present in the Bible. As stated in Wikipedia, "the work's depiction offers a free interpretation of the psychology of Jesus as a man and other characters. Much of the plot centers on Judas, who is dissatisfied with the direction in which Jesus is steering his disciples. Contemporary attitudes, sensibilities, and slang pervade the rock-opera's lyrics, and

ironic allusions to modern life are scattered throughout the depiction of political events."

So why did this production have such a profound impact on a 21-year old? First, the play depicts Jesus as a mortal, sexual, and flawed individual; even greedy for political power. This was not the Jesus I had been taught of in church and Bible school as the play took him off his pedestal as God and placed him on equal terms with me and the rest of the human race. Second, remembering this is "just" a play but also the Bible is "just" a book written by men/women as well, it was a view of God himself that I had never considered. Indeed, this play was part of my transition to becoming an atheist and rejecting the foolishness of my parent's strict Bible-based belief system. Of course, not everyone in the theater during those 771 productions became atheists. Many simply enjoyed the powerful music and story as told at face value. But then, I was going through a serious transition away from most of what I had learned as an adolescent including that at a Bible school. A Biblical quote seems relevant,

> "When I was a child, I spoke as a child, I understood as a child, I thought as a child: but when I became a man, I put away childish things."
>
> First Corinthians 13:11
>
> It appears that *Jesus Christ Superstar* helped me put away childish things.

VIGNETTE *18*

Transition to Adulthood: Building a New Person

JESUS CHRIST SUPERSTAR played an important part in my transitioning out of the strict religious belief model with prayer to Jesus for emotional support. Indeed, prayer, no matter how intense and belief based, accomplished nothing for me. I was becoming too much of a sceptic. While working in the Lundquist greenhouses, Dave could not understand why I was so transfixed with the music and text of *Jesus Christ Superstar*. Dave, no doubt, was a healthy normal and not as sensitive to the implications of lyrics that portrayed Jesus as a man.

When at bible college, I observed the "Christian warriors" (a hymn is titled "Onward Christian Soldiers") and decided many were late teen and early 20s brats. Their favorite derogatory designation for me was "cotton picker" to refer to African-American field workers. I do not remember why but it could have been because I liked wearing a silk smoking jacket in the dorm. I did not fit well into their social order and the school later isolated me in my own room in another building likely due to my various behavioral problems. These experiences along with those at home in Andover turned me vigorously against the society of Christian Fundamentalism.

When one is attempting to demolish their fundamental, foundational beliefs and devise a new person, it can be very traumatic. In addition to ADHD, PTSD and an anxiety disorder that I was unaware of at the time, I became seriously depressed and had suicidal ideations as discussed earlier and shown in my self-portrait. This is likely one of the reasons I was referred for psychotherapy, first to a Freudian Psychoanalyst and next, thankfully, to Dr. Marco Alfondary; the latter of whom came a decade later on my Lifeline. I was about to try and build a personal foundation on many psychopathologies just after leaving bible college and entering undergraduate school in Boston and this period ended with my first marriage.

In my early 20s I think I was experiencing a further stalling in development for at least three years, although it can last much longer. (Stalling during adolescence usually refers to delayed puberty, but this is not how I am using the term here.) For me this involved a depressive state and loss of personal direction. I simply did not know how to proceed in my life beyond professional activities. I appear to have had too little to work with; no sense of family, no parental guidance and a lack of the ability to establish strong personal relationships.

I have met a number of individuals who experienced developmental stalling that lasted much longer than three years as I use the term here. One of my girlfriends between marriages provides an example of how we can become stalled in development, possibly for our entire life. She experienced a dysfunctional marriage in her early 20s ending in an early divorce which left her, at age 35, still unable to relate, unable to move from the family fold and town where she grew up, and unable to work beyond her being in a small business with her sister; it is as though she simply stopped maturing in her 20s when she had her daughter and her husband left her. She even had slowed speech and difficulty communicating her thoughts, although the associated mannerisms were quite cute. It appears that many of these individuals live in the same house for their entire life, are unable to engage in challenging jobs due to anxiety and stress, and staying in the same town for life with the same or similar jobs. In my case, however, I had the counterbalancing forces of ADHD and mania to drive me forward as my 20s progressed to push me out of this stalled state.

Why does this matter to the psychiatrically challenged? There is a loss of productivity and lower income levels, introversion leads to fewer exploratory behaviors including social interactions and relationships, early and clinging to marital decisions, and an inability to go beyond their professional comfort zone. Adolescent abuse can evoke these types of conditions and spouses can provide protection for individuals suffering with chronic unresolved problems associated with adolescent abuse. I had withdrawn from my religious background, my parents were of no help as I recount below, marriage was an abysmal failure. For other individuals, alcohol and abuse of other drugs can delay adolescence.

My story diverges from most of those of other maltreated children; my many "sisters and brothers" as I call them in the broader sense of survivors of abuse. Instead of acting on the fantasy that I often experienced of going to Andover, MA and killing my parents, I struggled on with various psychopathologies in my late adolescence and explored how to spend the rest of my life as an undergraduate in Boston that produced more significant results scientifically than would have been produced by their deaths. I was fortunate to have a broad ranging educational exposure and met the late Dr. Helen Mahut, the "monkey lady" as she was called, when she was teaching a physiological psychology class. She studied memory following lesions (removal of bits of the brain) in monkeys until she was 90. I was so excited (transfixed) with such a prospect that I told her I would work in her lab doing the scut work like cleaning the animal cages just to continue learning from her. Having me wandering in her lab and looking for small jobs appears to have sent a shiver down her back. She quickly found me employment with Dr. Deepak N. Pandya at the Harvard Neurology Unit at Boston City Hospital. This also was a very fortunate outcome.

At this point I realized that brain research was the approach to understanding and possibly resolving my own pain and suffering. Obviously, it was stored in my brain and I thought the study of pain was crucial but was not yet aware of my ADHD and maltreatment as the actual causes of such internal strife. This is the fundamental point at which my story diverges from that of most of my "brothers and sisters."

Conclusions. I chose to build a new personality around neuroscience. Other adolescents often use vocal, visual or instrumental arts. Be it science, art, philosophy or even religion, moving from the context of abuse to one of a productive adult without stalling emotionally requires hard work and support from companions. Late adolescence usually involves terminating earlier living conditions and standards be it in college or a first job with apartment living. My experiences are not unique and, to the extent they were impaired by various forms of abuse, this makes the transition even more difficult as we carry this baggage in our brains from one context to another. It is my experience that recognizing previous abuse issues and one's personal strengths will enhance making it through this transitional period and the survivor's companions can play an important role therein.

VIGNETTE *19*

Marriage #1

MY FIRST WIFE was a full figured, blond who went to the same high school that I did in Andover and was in the same grade as I was. While a quick thinker, she had very little insight into herself and others as did I. She also had as little insight into sex as I did and its value in cementing emotional bonds as per her father's influence. Her father was a Ford salesman and scallywag who brought women home for sexual interludes. His wife simply went along with the program and overlooked his proclivities for other women. Of course, he could provide his daughter Joyce with no relevant model of interpersonal interactions that joined sex and emotional bonds as he was a high-impact fornicator himself. Thus, here we have two young adults Joyce and myself engaged in a dysfunctional relationship that neither of us understood. While she was getting a masters degree in social work, we spent our weekends together in bed mostly exchanging bodily fluids without an understanding of sex and how it relates to a love relationship. I am not certain that we even loved each other.

It is still unclear why we married; two lost souls who had no interest in forming a family or other shared interpersonal bonds. My late adolescent years were spent entirely in Boston and this is the town I lived in for more than a decade and identified as home. We were married in the Boston Museum of Fine Arts, which was forbidden but that did not produce any constraints for an individual with ADHD who was

Marriage #1

used to breaking boundaries. Thus, we had a justice of the peace and two friends as witnesses join us in the museum for a brief ceremony under Gauguin's painting *"Where Do We Come From? What Are We? Where Are We Going?"* How appropriate for someone who had gone through a major personal transformation. One would not call this a traditional wedding with no parents or in-laws present; what did we know of family?

After our wedding in the museum, we had a bottle of bubbly to celebrate this confused undertaking and I stripped and took a swim in the very dirty Charles River; at this time it had not yet been cleaned up like it is today. Remember the Scanells' song "Dirty water" which in part includes the words

> "Yeah, down by the river
> Down by the banks of the river Charles
> (Aw, that's what's happenin' baby)
> That's where you'll find me
> Along with lovers, muggers, and thieves
> (Aw, but they're cool people)
> well I love that dirty water
> Oh, Boston, you're my home"

We lived in various apartments in Boston. At one point I had a pet corn snake that would slither around my neck. Snakes do not provide the emotional engagement of a puppy and you had to be careful if you had fed it an egg that as the egg worked its way through its digestive system, there was a point where it had to be released and one did not want the snake on their neck when that happened. On another occasion I had a Capuchin monkey, also called an organ grinder monkey because they would accompany their master on the streets of Boston helping them beg for money. Eventually, the monkey had to be given away because it would rip everything in the apartment apart including the closets and the cage was too small for such an animal. Once again, these experiences recall difficulties in cognitive judgements by

The ADHD and Abuse-Damaged Brain

an owner with ADHD. Finally, Joyce and I settled into a Florida-style condominium in Weymouth, MA on the 56th floor with a porch and great view of Boston. I was going to graduate school at the time for a degree in anatomy and neurobiology. Joyce actually thought I was going to become a neurosurgeon. When she explicitly heard this was not the case, you could visibly see her enthusiasm for our marriage falter. It is unclear what she expected except possibly the good life on the salary of a neurosurgeon.

Joyce was not happy after a few years and, at a professional meeting, she met with a colleague who gave her marijuana and engaged in sex with her. This seemed to be very much more to her liking than her current marital status which I suspect still evoked a bit of guilt even for her. At a group party in our condominium one night there was much conversation about sex and this is the second to the last time I saw her. She had wanted to go to couples therapy which we did. However, she met individually with the group leader and left his office and the group with a sneer on her face to me that I never understood. We were divorced in 1978. She eventually went bankrupt and died at the age of 56 in 2003. Although she could have contracted cancer, I assume her death was due to her proclivities for casual sex that was discussed at the above party. She may have acquired the Human Immunodeficiency virus that causes Acquired Immune Deficiency Syndrome (AIDS). This epidemic began in the 1980s and hit its peak in mortality in 1997 and was untreatable at the time.

There is no record of her demise or obituary as she had developed no intimate relationships with people concerned with her life. A sad end to a life that could have achieved much more but her sexual proclivities likely got in the way of her accomplishing anything of significance with her life.

Summary and suggestions. While I am not a marriage counselor, I have observed many of them. My first effort at this activity was a confused relationship based on sex that was uninformed by a strong emotional connection or any shared goals. In retrospect, as a Fundamentalist Christian untrained in the ways of sex, I have always been surprised at the role that meeting the sexual needs of your partner play in fulfilling a marriage; but then my family downplayed, sex, dancing, movies, and rock and roll, i.e., all the fun stuff. I don't need to tell people that are married that shared goals are a critical part of a lifetime relationship. Indeed, in my second effort at marriage, it was almost immediately stated that we wanted to have two children and live in rural settings as well as work together in the field of neuroscience. Apparently I had learned some lessons from my first marriage.

VIGNETTE
20

Adventure in the Northwest Territories

I TOOK A *trip to the Northwest Territories in late July and early August at age 35 between marriages. The Northwest Territories is a sparsely populated Canadian province and Yellowknife is its capital city. At first it was just for the physical challenge but it had other consequences. It changed my perspectives on myself and life in general. It had a very calming effect on my mentality as it was not only challenging but I also interacted with no other human companion and reached my peak physical condition at this time.*

I took my 750cc Suzuki motorcycle on the road to Yellowknife at the time when it was only mud covered (see plate of pictures). My 365 pound motorcycle loaded with 150 pounds of gear fell over three times and it took quite an effort to get about a quarter of a ton upright; particularly in the slippery mud. Passing truckers looking down and watching me found this quite humorous. A pontoon plane in Yellowknife took me 150 miles north and I selected an island from the air that I would stay on until leaving three weeks later. Here I set up camp, fished for lake trout (see the picture) and target practiced with my .458 caliber bolt-action rifle in case I met bears on the trip back; many scats and footprints alerted to their presence. After seeing how long it took to reload for a second shot for a lefty with a rifle built for right-handed

Adventure in the Northwest Territories

riflemen, I decided that if I just injured it I was a dead man because I could not get a second shot. Instead I decided to role up in a ball and let it have its way with me. Fortunately, this was not necessary.

During the three hour night, thousands of mice would appear and were quite friendly as they had never seen such a visitor before. They also enjoyed finishing my supper by climbing into my cooking dish. When the sun appeared, they quickly went into their nests as birds of prey such as owls are their nemesis. On another evening the sky lit up like an ominous fire (pictured). I did not know that this was a warning of a pending storm and later my friends and I were to be in a most ferocious storm with very high winds, rain and extensive lightning strikes that were actually quite frightening. This amazing time, however, came to an end and, while I had to say goodbye to my friends, the adventure was far from over.

I had never been in a canoe on a river before which I planned to follow with maps. I got my first important lesson on the first river after leaving my campsite because the maps did not have changes marked where beavers had reengineered the river's course and intensity. Coming around the first bend in the river I was confronted with fallen trees and gushing water currents that I could not navigate around. The canoe slammed sideways up against the trees and bumped wildly against them. I emptied the canoe by climbing over the trees, pulled the canoe out of the water and away from the small waterfall that followed. This taught me to listen for waterfalls, pull the canoe out of the water when I heard them, check them and, if non-negotiable, portage around them. In some instances this required dragging the canoe and its contents up to one mile usually through dense underbrush. The pictured rapids are an example of where I misjudged their intensity and was thrown from the canoe with all of my belongings that were tightly sealed in plastic bags. I don't have a picture of one fork in a river that led to 5 standing waves and threw me again. I had never seen such river formations much less trying to navigate through them in a canoe.

When I returned from this trip my physical condition was at its peak but I also felt like a renewed person. I was mentally calm and free of the pressures of modern day society. It also helped me look inside myself in a way not possible before with the drone of everyday life.

Conclusions. While this experience started as a personal challenge, it shows a number of additional things. First, I was willing to cross boundaries and engage in activities without a high degree of planning and fear of going it alone and trying things I had never done before as would be expected for a person with ADHD. I was completely self-dependent. Second, it had a profound impact on my mental well-being that I had not expected. The trip from the island via poorly marked and beaver reengineered rivers and onto numerous lakes with overgrown river outlets produced an intense daily struggle particularly with three capsizing experiences in which all belongings were at risk. The stress of trying to avoid waterfalls helped me develop concentration and self-discipline. The experience significantly changed my mental state for about two years thereafter.

VIGNETTE *21*

Psychotherapy: Marco, BPD and DBT

IT WAS SUGGESTED by a graduate school counselor that I engage with a psychotherapist to work on the issues that were bothering me and this is what I did at around 21 years of age. Apparently the therapist was of the Freudian Psychoanalytic School of thought as she sat quietly through each 50 minute session diligently taking notes while I laid bare my soul. She never said anything, never suggested possible alternatives to alleviating my suffering or drew conclusions about how to handle the internal struggles presented to her. I guess this is being non-judgmental in its extreme. This seemed odd to me as I did not understand how this "therapy" would accomplish anything. In other words, it seemed to me that I was in the same place mentally week after week. After 9 months of her complete silence, I stood up in front of her at her desk (yes there was a desk between her and me) and told her that this exercise was pointless and that it appears I would have to go out into the world to understand and solve my problems myself. She in no way defended her approach; her face was blank. This, of course, was a rather bold statement on my part but the next 50 years and maybe more were dedicated to such an undertaking and this volume summarizes many of my difficulties and insights.

Dr. Marco Alfondary. Here we move forward on my Lifeline by about one decade. The late Dr. Marco Alfondary had a robust and vivacious personality and provided the inverse of my previous psychoanalytic experience. He was a dynamic and excited psychotherapist that relished getting into someone's head and addressing their issues with a frontal assault by challenging presumed life precepts. This was exactly what I needed versus a passive and virtually mute therapist. He helped me to lance the wounds in my brain and emit some of the psychiatric puss that had built up there in over three decades. When I arrived for each therapy session, he was already to go; he would lean forward in his chair (no desk was between us), look me straight in the eyes with great intensity and was anxious to hear what was on the day's menu. He was a no-nonsense, up front therapist who did not hold back on the difficult issues; in fact he relished them. He clearly was completely engaged in our experience together.

Marco marked a turning point in my life and so I show his picture here taken a few years later with my 8 month old boy Lukas in the Boston Commons with a Swan Boat behind them. During our sessions, we did not talk in terms of grand theories of psychotherapy but rather addressed my everyday problems. My struggles with anger for my first wife, which was still an open wound, my difficulty relating to other women and professional issues seemed to disappear without a conscious effort to resolve them. I attribute some of the resolution of my abuse experiences to Marco. He made it possible for me to break the wall (religious jail cell if you would) and move on to my second marriage and raising two children. As such, he is a key point in my Lifeline. I stated before and will again that I hope each abuse survivor finds their Marco as soon as possible to have him/her help to drain the swamp that collects in our brains.

Lessons from My Daughter. When Emily was 8 she confirmed my view that I have ADHD with her diagnosis using current assessment tools. It was likely that many of my emotional and behavioral adolescent difficulties were generated by this syndrome and it is likely that I am the one that may have transmitted ADHD genes to her. Emily emphasized that many of the difficulties I had in growing up were ADHD based; delays in emotional, cognitive and social interaction development. She was vulnerable to an online predator whose activities led her to severe emotional disruption including "cutting" as a form of self-harm. For a time she was prescribed either Ritalin or Vyvanse. Eventually this led us both to Dialectical Behavioral Therapy. Unfortunately, I was not yet fully aware of the concept of emotional abuse to which she is very sensitive and this will be considered at the end of Vignette 32.

Dialectical Behavioral Therapy (DBT). I must briefly move forward on my Lifeline to consider DBT as it may be a viable form of psychotherapy for abuse survivors, Borderline Personality Disorder (BPD) and ADHD. These disorders share symptoms that feature impulsive behavior, emotional dysregulation including difficulties in controlling anger and aggression, attention deficits and those in decision making. Repeated non-suicidal self-injury and suicidal behavior are typical patterns of emotional and behavioral dysregulation. Ferrer and colleagues (2017; *European Journal of Psychiatry and Neuroscience*, volume 267, pages 541-549) reported an association between experiencing traumatic events in childhood and a higher clinical severity of BPD in adulthood. A history of physical trauma in childhood could be associated with the persistence of ADHD in adulthood and emotional or sexual abuse with later development of BPD or comorbid BPD-ADHD. Given these profiles, I may have suffered with BPD as shown in the picture "Hands" in Vignette 16, although I did not actually engage in cutting but my daughter did and she was so diagnosed. I also expressed suicidal behavior during my Transition Period and, my impulsivity and to a lesser extent aggression, are well demonstrated. My lifetime with ADHD would have clearly enhanced the negative outcomes associated with BPD.

There are hundreds of studies over the past two decades reporting that comorbid ADHD and BPD are frequent versus patients with ADHD alone. The comorbid group express high levels of impulsivity, aggression, novelty seeking and conduct problems, cognitive and psychosocial impairments and anxiety, somatoform, Bipolar Disorder (BD), PTSD and major depression just to name a few. What is DBT?

A parent is usually "encouraged" to participate with their adolescent and, given my many mental maladies, I was chosen for this activity which actually did Emily and me a world of good. DBT is a form of cognitive-behavioral therapy that attempts to identify and change negative thinking patterns and pushes for positive behavioral changes. DBT may be used to treat suicidal and other self-destructive behaviors some of which are associated with BPD and associated self-injury via cutting usually of the arm. It teaches patients skills to cope with, and change, unhealthy behaviors. The term "dialectical" refers to bringing together two opposites in therapy - acceptance and change – that produces better results than either one alone. A unique aspect of DBT is its focus on acceptance of a patient's experience as a way for therapists to reassure them and balance the work needed to change negative behaviors.

Methylphenidate (Ritalin) is often given to adolescents with ADHD as was the case for Emily. Importantly, it also improves the outcomes of DBT for patients with comorbid ADHD and BPD (Prada and colleagues; 2015; *ADHD Attention Deficit and Hyperactivity Disorder*, volume 7, pages 199-209). This combination of therapies should be considered.

As a neuroscientist, however, I must ask if DBT actually alters brain structure and/or function and is not simply based on a belief system that makes the patients feel good. Indeed, there is objective data that supports the ability of DBT to change brain structures in places that mediate emotional and to some extent cognitive functions including, but not restricted to, cingulate cortex.

Mancke and colleagues (2018; *Journal of Psychiatry and Neuroscience*, volume 43, issue 3, pages 171-181) evaluated female patients with BPD before and after participation in 12 weeks of residential DBT and compared them to female patients with BPD who only received treatment as usual. Patients receiving DBT showed an *increase* in the volume of anterior cingulate cortex (ACC) that mediates emotional functions and the anterior midcingulate (aMCC) and to a

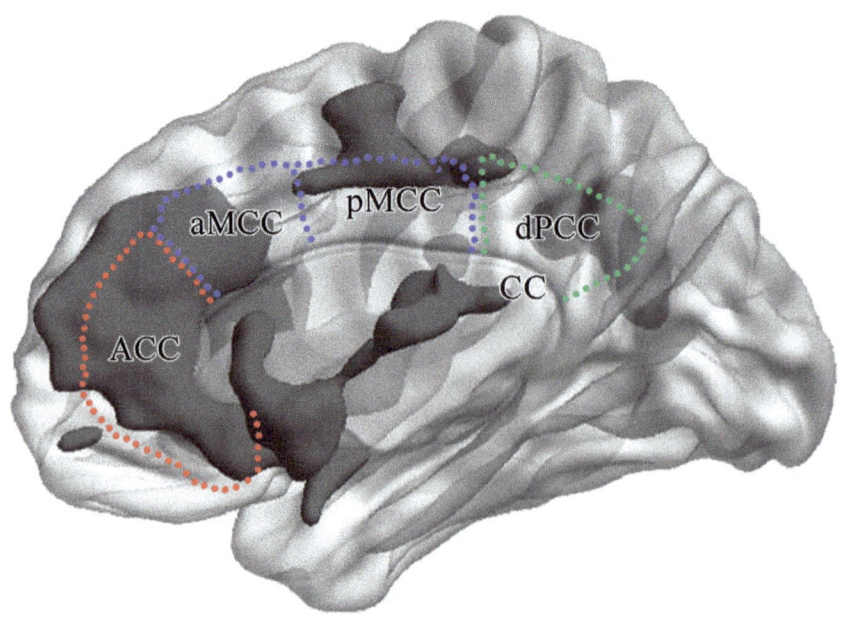

lesser extent posterior midcingulate cortices; the latter two of which are involved in cognitive, mental and motor functions. This picture shows the medial surface of the right hemisphere from this study that I relabeled and the intensity of grey shading reflects the DBT-generated *increases* in cortical volume.

Thus, DBT evokes organic brain changes that improve emotional and cognitive functions. These changes may be further amplified with Ritalin providing a powerful therapeutic approach to ADHD and BPD. If a parent has a child suffering with BPD and possibly ADHD, I recommend DBT as it evokes organic changes in brain function. Emily and I are both in a better place today after DBT and she is starting to blossom as a fine young person. I have consciously stopped emotionally abusing her in the Cycle of Violence and the future is quite bright for both of us.

Let me finish with a "P.S." on one of Emily's recent Father's Day cards. "We have gone through a lot of rough times, and we both got hurt. But I think we will be stronger after all of this. I remember all of the good moments we had. I love you so much."

VIGNETTE **22**

Empathy

EMPATHY UNDERLIES MUCH in the way of social interactions and I have always wondered why I am so deficient therewith. With this vignette, I have finally arrived at an explanation as to why I am so impaired in this function; major damage to my MCC. Empathy refers to sharing the emotions of others and is central to successful socializing. It is the ability to understand what others feel, be it an emotion or a sensory state. Accordingly, empathic experience enables us to understand what it feels like when someone else experiences sadness or happiness, and also pain or touch and is associated with activation in neural structures that are also active during the first-hand experience of that emotion. For example, cutaneous (skin) pain activates mainly MCC (Vignette 2) and this is one of the parts of the brain involved in pain empathy; i.e., part of the neural activity shared between self- and other-related experiences.

Singer and colleagues (2004; *Science*, volume 303, pages 1157-1162) reported that actual pain to oneself mainly activates aMCC (coded red in the picture below), while observing the pain in another person (a loved one in this instance) activated mainly pMCC (coded green). There are two sites in each cingulate region where the red and green overlap but the meaning of this is still unclear; they may be associated with co-ordinating responses between the two regions. Also, other parts of the brain are engaged in empathy, not just cingulate cortex.

Empathy

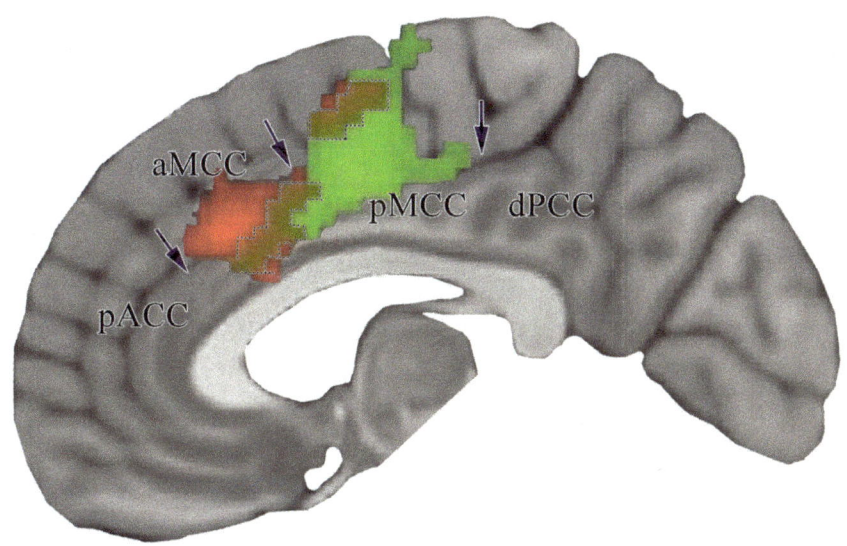

Thus, if we observe someone in pain, this response helps us respond to the other person's pain in a caring manner as we would our own pain. Also, empathy helps a social group to share experiences that are helpful to survival. An example is that of a monkey troop that is threatened by an intruder and they coalesce as a group for protection in what is termed "emotional contagion." The behavior of humans during a mass shooting incident suggests that a similar response is at work.

I have always had a limited concern for the internal intensions and struggles of others and this has caused difficulties with family and colleague interactions. I propose for the first time in this vignette that the parts of my brain including MCC are disrupted by so many psychopathologies (ADHD, 3 forms of abuse, anxiety, BPD, and BD) that empathy is seriously impaired in my brain. In other words my MCC along with a few other parts of my brain are shrunken and dysfunctional and block my empathic responses. This was pronounced in many instances during my second marriage when empathy was expected but not present. Let us consider a few examples.

When early arriving in Boston my second wife had an accident on the Massachusetts Turnpike. While I asked how the car was, my graduate student, who became a neurologist, was concerned with whether or not she was hurt. He expressed empathy, I did not. In another instance our unborn son was leaking amniotic fluid and Leslie was put on bed rest for two weeks. Each day I would make her a peanut butter sandwich with a glass of water and go to work. Not a very caring response to her situation, i.e., virtually no empathy for her condition. On another occasion, when she clearly had a severe fever and had not yet recovered, I asked, can you go to work now? Hmmm, really! Somewhat later when she was still pregnant and I was going to London to do pain research, I wanted her to be protected in our home in the woods of North Carolina. For this I got out my .458 caliber, bolt action Winchester rifle, also known as an elephant gun, that weighed quite a bit and, if not held carefully, could dislocate one's shoulder. Expert hunters have at times been thrown to the ground by such a rifle. My pregnant wife could hardly hold it up much less fire it so we nixed this idea and still laugh about such an absurd effort to this day. Even when my daughter hit a deer recently I was mainly concerned about the car rather than her condition. Empathy I did not have, but I am consciously working on it.

Interestingly, at this time I am capable of sadness for others particularly when watching tough movies such as "Schindler's List" and "What's Love Got to Do with It". Sadness may involve empathy; e.g., two times I could not watch the former movie past the part where a Nazi guard kills a worker by shooting him in the head on the street and this evokes crying. Thus, there may be a different system in the brain for sadness that is not linked to empathy or extreme levels of sadness break through even my weak empathy system.

Summary and Suggestions. One of the recurring messages of my experiences is that psychiatric diseases usually do not come in simple boxes, one at a time and in separate and unrelated places in the brain but rather generate complex and summating interactions; ADHD, abuse, PTSD, anxiety, BD and BPD disorders were a few of the diseases that I was coping with throughout my life that summated to impair midcingulate functions. This interferes with social interactions and empathy. The message for readers including survivors of harsh abuse and various genetic disorders such as ADHD is that it is necessary to find a therapist who is well-versed in your problem; i.e., that fits your specific needs. If the first or second choices do not work out, consider other therapeutic approaches such as hypnosis, biofeedback, relaxation and various forms of cognitive-behavioral therapy. Drug therapy in combination with these approaches should also be considered in the normal course of treatment as none of these approaches may truly "work" for vulnerable survivors of harsh abuse. The sooner you find your "Marco" the better. Finally, one can expect that the cascade of neurological impairments will be additive in the brain to impair other functions such as empathy. I am still working on this issue and it can be solved, although slowly. Thus, it is important to document all of one's impairments to determine if their cumulative effects are themselves causing further serious problems.

VIGNETTE
23

Neuro-Psycho-Pharmacology

NOW THAT IS a mouthful; a long word with three parts that are not hyphenated. "Neuro-" stands for neuron or brain, "psycho-" for mind or brain function and "pharmacology" for the study of drug actions in the brain and the treatment of brain disorders with drugs. Altogether it means the study of drug actions in the brain and their use for treating brain disorders. Reconsider the second picture in Vignette 1 that summarizes my various psychopathologies and treatments late in my adult life most of which involve drug therapies.

Even before engaging with a psychotherapist, I was well aware of my mental difficulties from two perspectives in my early 20s. First, I was depressed during the year or so after completely breaking my ties with my cold religious family and this continues to today as part of my Bipolar Disorder (BD; manic/depressive swings). I used to say that I was going to recreate a person from the ground up. I even patterned my signature after John Hancock's because people would ask me for my John Hancock; so I gave it to them. During one depressive time I would walk through the traffic around Copley Square in the hopes of being hit. Given the proclivities of Boston drivers to overlook pedestrians and any other obstacle in their way, this had to be a sure-fire way to commit suicide by automobile; obviously it did not work. The second way I knew there was something amiss in my brain were the particularly intense (manic) work phases that came on in the form of a Spring mania. This was quite obvious in my data collection in graduate school as during April and May in particular I acquired and analyzed the greatest amount of data. I would work until 2 or 3 AM drawing neurons with jazz, blues or classical music playing on the radio or recoding the chatter of neurons as I stimulated their inputs in cingulate slices and listened with an audio recording device to hear their activity. I now realize that I was benefitting from my ADHD and too some extent from BD symptoms. Indeed, those of us that can channel our "deficits" productively can outperform our competitors. When untreated, however, BD comes with associated behavioral risks.

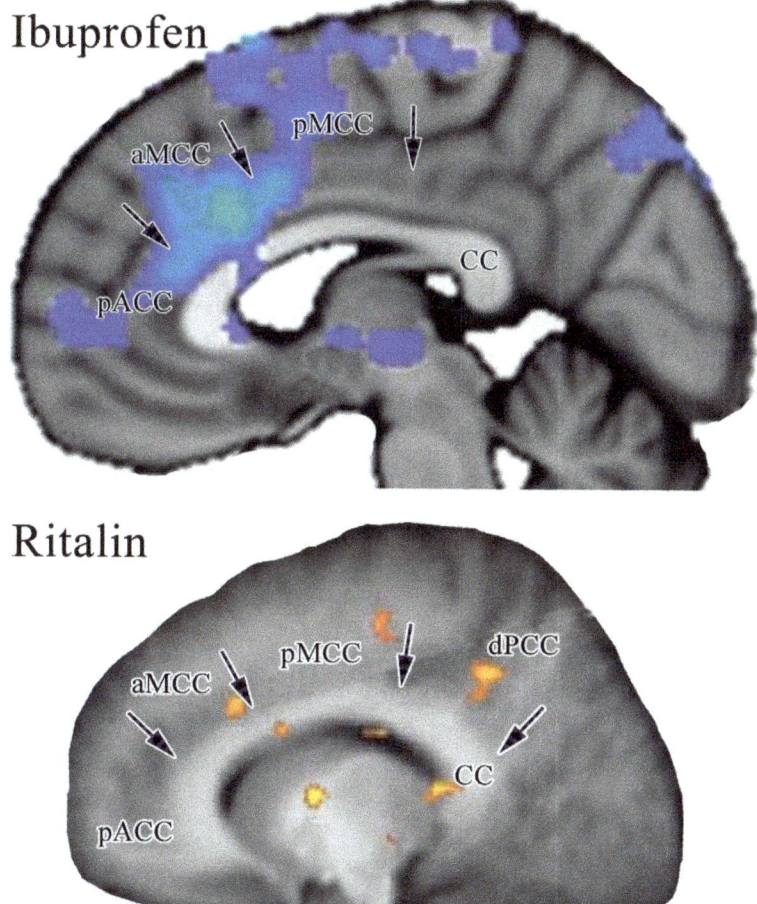

Drugs often have actions in the peripheral muscles, joints, gut and skin but also in the brain including cingulate cortex. Neuroscientists attempt to target brain areas that are engaged in specific functional disorders. Drugs seek out their receptors where their actions are focused, I have selected two examples to show the actions of drugs in this regard with the images for each shown in the picture above. In the first is the response to a drug that most everyone will recognize as it is widely used for pain relief; ibuprofen (also termed a non-steroidal anti-inflammatory drug). Hodkinson and colleagues (2015; *Pain*, volume 156, issue 7, pages 1301-1310) showed that ibuprofen *reduces* activity mainly in aMCC but also to a lesser extent in pACC and pMCC following third molar extractions. Not surprisingly, this is the region where greatest pain activity is observed in cingulate cortex (third picture in Vignette 2; top right). The second drug is Ritalin which is often prescribed for ADHD in adolescents and adults. It additionally appears to improve the effectiveness of Dialectical Behavioral Therapy. Bush and colleagues (2008; *Archives of General Psychiatry*, volume 65, issue 1, pages 102-114) evaluated ADHD patients taking Ritalin (also termed methylphenidate) while performing a cognitive task and showed activity in aMCC and dPCC. As the patients were engaged in a behavioral task, these sites are likely not as extensive as might be expected without the task. Thus, we have evidence that two drugs with well-known effects have activity in aMCC; i.e., their effects are organically based and not a matter of belief systems or the placebo effect.

Turning back to my experiences, I never wanted to impair the positive features of my disorders as an adult so I was averse to drug therapy. That was actually a bad decision, particularly in a family setting. As you will note later on my Lifeline, there is a reference to anxiety and citalopram (also Celexa). My introduction to psychoactive drugs was with this drug prescribed by an alert primary care physician later in my life who recognized my anxiety disorder just after we moved to Upstate, NY. Interestingly, this drug enhances the presence of a brain chemical termed serotonin and is often prescribed for depression but also eating disorders, panic disorder, and social phobia. One of the places in the brain it is most active is subgenual anterior cingulate cortex (sACC) in the limbic system. Consider again in Vignette 2 the localizing effects of stress (PTSD) and abuse. In order for a drug to be effective, it must "seek out" those areas in the brain that are damaged and responsible for particular deficits.

Being well versed in the details of *offensive* driving during my years in Boston, these "talents" continued while in Upstate. One aspect is impatiently driving to a goal with little interest in what else is happening except in order to avoid serious accidents. One of the hallmarks of ADHD is difficulty keeping one's mind on the task at hand and not being distracted by other internal thoughts. That spells trouble for teens and adults when they're behind the wheel of a vehicle. Studies show that people with ADHD are more likely to speed, have accidents, and lose their drivers' licenses. During the first weeks on citalopram, I recall driving to work but for some reason the pressure was greatly reduced. I was actually driving at the speed limit and was not bothered by waiting for other drivers. This was an amazing observation for a Boston driver; I was being patient in traffic. For the first time I asked myself, "is this what it is like to be normal?" Citalopram was reducing my stress levels in sACC.

This drug had a significant impact on my mental health and I took it for a few years but I was later prescribed clonazepam which to this day is very effective. I should mention that taking these drugs in limited amounts did not dull my work as a professional neuroscientist as I had expected. In addition, my family found me much more agreeable on citalopram and it had a significant impact on all relationships; committee meetings were also more bearable and I was able to contribute in a more productive and less disruptive manner.

In view of my two subsequent mental breakdowns and other problems such as depression associated with Bipolar Disorder (BD), I was placed on Depakote/valproate. This drug also has been effective. On two occasions I slowly weaned myself off of it to see if my wife would notice and determine that it was really necessary. She noticed that I had stopped taking it as I became more irritable and anxious and I have been taking it ever since. At high doses, however, Depakote itself can evoke intention tremors (shaking of one or both hands when performing detailed activities); however, at half dose it has ameliorated my BD and the intension tremors are resolved.

Finally, it is the effectiveness of various drugs, as well as other behavioral factors and a few professional diagnoses, that as an adult I can claim to have the particular disorders shown in the second picture in Vignette 1. If nicotine, clonazepam and Depakote were not effective, it would have been more likely that I did not suffer with the various disorders enumerated there. Thus, drug responses have predictive value in assessing one's psychiatric issues and a diagnosis alone may not be adequate.

VIGNETTE
24

The Dawn of Modern Neuroscience and a Key Discovery

THE 1970S WERE a time of great excitement in the brain sciences. The relationships between anatomy, physiology, behavior and neurology were becoming apparent to the point where integration was possible in ways not previously conceived. One could study brain circuits, individual neurons, drug binding sites where they function, behavioral alterations following lesions and small, localized strokes. Almost anything one touched at this time was new and exciting. This was the dawn of modern neuroscience.

In undergraduate school, Dr. Helen Mahut found me a job working for Dr. Depack N. Pandya in the Harvard Neurology Unit at Boston City Hospital (BCH). The unit was run by a brilliant neurologist, the late Dr. Norman Geschwind, who's major publications were reproduced by Orrin Devinsky and Steven C. Schachter in a book titled *"Norman Geschwind: Selected Publications on Language, Behavior and Epilepsy"* (no longer available due to its popularity). He held his neurology clinic on the 9th floor of BCH and was a rare clinical neurologist due to his insights into brain diseases. One could give him a set of symptoms; he would think for a few moments and then tell you where in the brain the patient had suffered a stroke. These predictions were often confirmed on postmortem analyses of the patient's brains. This was a very important talent at the time as we did not have accurate brain imaging techniques to localize brain damage. He was intensely focused and inquisitive and this latter characteristic led him to realize how important basic research was to any further progress in the field. When the unit was disbanded to go across town to Beth Israel Hospital, I was given some of the wall hangings that he used in his teaching.

The Denny-Brown Research Laboratories were located on the 10th floor of BCH. In addition to wet bench laboratories and offices, there was a surgical suite and housing for about two dozen rhesus monkeys. My office was just off the surgical suite and the two monkey rooms were across the hall. When an investigator walked into the monkey rooms, they would hold onto the front bars of their cages with all four feet and shake them as hard as they could all the while cackling and squealing to each other to alert that there was an intruder present just as a monkey troop would do in the wild when an intruder appeared. I think this was great fun for them as they gestured with their faces and bobbed their heads back and forth as though to threaten you. Otherwise, for most of the day, they ate apples, played with occasional toys and themselves by masturbating.

One day a very large monkey with large canines got away from a resident and entered the stairwell. I was on the top floor looking down; the resident's face was frantic and blanched white as he tried to recapture the monkey at the end of a long stick with a retractable sling on it. The difficulty was that there were swinging doors to all the patient corridors up and down this stairwell and none were locked. One can only imagine the confusion and angst that would have ensued had this large beast started a rampage down one of the patient corridors. Fortunately for the poor resident, he was able to capture the animal and get it back into his cage (the monkey's cage not the resident's).

I cannot resist telling one more story from what I observed in the surgical suite. This was at a time before Institutional Animal Care and Use Committees (IACUCs) were established with very strict animal handling and use rules and veterinarian oversight. A postdoctoral fellow was operating on an anesthetized monkey and he had injected Mannitol (a sugar) into its blood to remove water from the brain so that it would shrink and he could access the part of the brain he wanted to analyze. As it takes about 30-45 minutes for Mannitol to act, he decided to take a smoking brake. Not unreasonable until you realize that all the surgical instruments and the head of the monkey were sterilized with alcohol which is quite flammable. As he leaned over the head of the animal puffing on his cigarette, a fire broke out on the animal's cranium; the brain had not yet been exposed. As the light blue flame danced on the monkey's head, the postdoc picked up a few wads of gauze and gently patted the animal's head with it. When the fire had been extinguished, he turned to me and, with something of a swagger in his voice, pointed out that he had never had an infection in one of his animals. Hmmm; was that because of the alcohol or fire? We will never know.

The entire 10 floor BCH building has since been demolished along with its many memories and the Boston City Medical Center has been completely transformed. I should also note that most primate research is now performed at regional primate centers around the country. There will be no more cranial fires during monkey neurosurgical procedures or the risk of large, ferocious monkeys with robust canines charging down patient halls.

The neurology unit was a wonderful environment in which all who participated flourished. Dr. Norman Geschwind single handedly trained the next generation of neurologists and many scientists that Dr. Pandya recruited went on to become world leaders in primate neuroanatomy. It was in this environment that I was blessed to have entered after completing my baccalaureate degree at Northeastern University. Dr. Mahut had engineered a win/win situation; she did not have to deal with the horror of having Brent wandering freely around her lab cleaning rat cages and Dr. Pandya got a very intense and productive assistant. This is an instance where my ADHD really paid off. No one was more engaged in brain research than I was; they simply did not have my "disorder." Dr. Pandya and I would sit over a double-viewing microscope and ponder, for the first time, the meaning of specific somatosensory connections to brain function. To do so we would finger change in our pockets to observe what went into somatic sensation and how these connections might contribute to sensory discrimination.

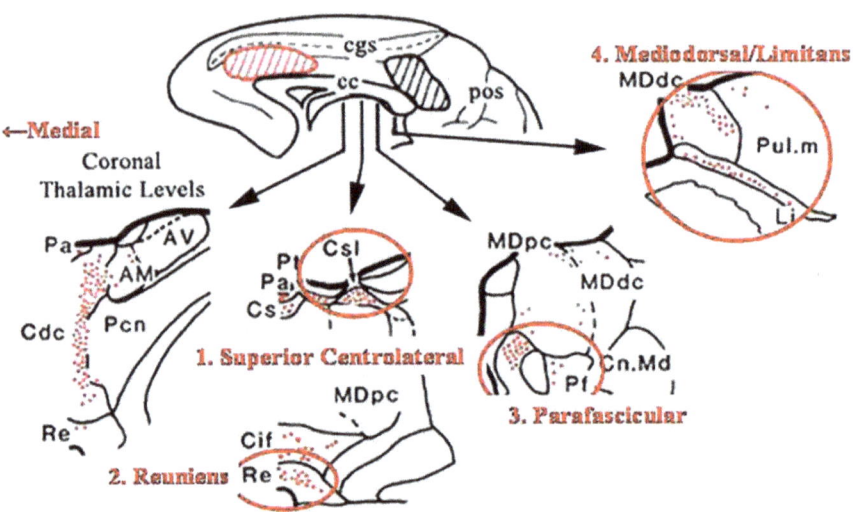

I shall describe but one of my studies while at the Neurology Unit because of its impact on me and the field of neuroscience in general. It also exemplifies the excitement of innovative scientific exploration. At the time we were using a molecule to study connections in the monkey brain. One would inject this enzyme into the region of interest and neurons with inputs to that region would pick it up and transport it to cell bodies throughout the brain. Of course, I was studying cingulate cortex with it. The accepted line of thinking was that cingulate cortex received inputs from what is termed the "limbic thalamus" that included mainly the anterior and mediodorsal nuclei (see Vignette 2 for where the thalamus is located).

One fateful Saturday in a quiet microscopy room in the Harvard Neurology Unit at Beth Israel Hospital that had recently moved from BCH, I was searching to see if this "principle" of brain connectivity was actually true. In this figure one of the injections was in the back part of cingulate cortex (black hatched area; do not worry about all the detailed labeling) and indeed neurons were labeled with the marker in the anterior and mediodorsal nuclei as predicted. *However*, while there were a few such neurons following an injection into the anterior part of cingulate cortex (red hatched area), I came across large patches of labelled neurons in what are called the intralaminar, mediodorsal and midline thalamic nuclei (red dots stand for 3-5 labeled neurons). Starting from the front of the brain and working back I would put a slide under the microscope and, seeing these neurons but not many in the other nuclei became so excited that I could not sit still so I had to get up and walk around the room to settle down before going on to the next slide. No one had reported such a finding and I was aware of Dr. Kenneth Casey's studies at the National Institute of Mental Health reporting that when he applied a painful stimulus to a monkey's skin, it would drive these neurons to respond. For the first time I was studying the source of pain-responding neurons in cingulate cortex!

The slide review went on all day and my excitement grew with each passing slide. Clearly the dogma about cingulate thalamic input was only partially correct and I had found the source of painful inputs to it. Indeed, neurosurgeons removed this part of cingulate cortex to relieve chronic cancer pain, there was a high level of opioid (morphine) binding in this region (see our logo in the next vignette) and it was involved in emotion (we now know it is mainly fear activity). All the parts of a new story were in place and we published this study in the journal *Science* in 1979 when other scientists thought that pain was mainly due to activity in the somatosensory system. Surprisingly, they had no concept of the role of emotion in pain. At that point I decided to study cingulate cortex because I thought pain processing in the brain was the source of my suffering from my adolescent abuse and would be solved by studying this region. About 35 years later I realized that it was not pain *per se* but rather harsh physical abuse that evokes mental pain and stress that would become and is to this day my primary concern.

I made this shift in focus to harsh physical abuse when in North Carolina because of a study we published with a group of gastroenterologists of a woman that was raped between the ages of 4 and 7 by a family "friend." She developed irritable bowel syndrome that resolved spontaneously but it returned with severe abdominal pain after she married an abusive husband in her early 20s. At this time I decided to spend about 12 years developing an animal model of physical abuse that could be used to study how brain chemicals change under such circumstances. While human imaging has much value in such studies, the timing, intensity and duration of abuse are virtually impossible to match from one individual to another. Socioeconomic factors that influence abuse responses in humans are not experienced by experimental animals removing a significant variable, animals bred for research are genetically similar and their brains are available for analysis; human subjects do not to give us their brains for detailed studies. The value of experimental animal research to such work is considered in the last vignette.

Conclusions. In this vignette I report the excitement of the scientific process and how it led me to study cingulate cortex using mainly monkeys in the early years. This work has now transitioned to analysis of pain and stress in the context of physical abuse. It has been a long journey with many ups and downs particularly in finding support for such work. The concept of harsh physical abuse tends to put off healthy normal individuals who could provide support; clearly it is a horrifying and unpleasant subject to discuss abuse much less study it. However, driven by ADHD, mania and my own abuse experiences; it is not yet over as we continue to go beyond our first experimental study, now using rabbits, that show alterations in cingulate cortex following physical abuse. Additionally, we have shifted the focus of Cingulum Neurosciences Institute to one of primarily understanding the mechanisms of abuse.

VIGNETTE
25

Founding of Cingulum Neurosciences Institute

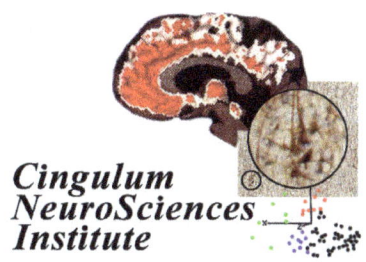

TO THE EXTENT that one is truly innovative and not willing to fit into the boxes created by healthy normals, there are times when alternative routes around the healthy scientists are required. One of these routes for me was in the founding of Cingulum Neurosciences Institute (CNSI). There were two reasons for forming a non-profit corporation in 1997 around the motif of the structure, connections, functions and diseases of cingulate cortex; at face value an odd undertaking indeed. I am often asked, "How do you make money at such an activity?" That is a very good question and not a month goes by when I do not ask it myself as we do not make much in the way of revenue or donations.

Our logo is shown above and it has three parts. The top picture is of my brain with the distribution of opioid binding coded in red with the most in ACC and aMCC, less in pMCC and least in dPCC. The middle picture is of large pyramidal-shaped neurons with dendrites emitted from their apex. The bottom picture is from one of our studies of Alzheimer's disease that showed there are possibly five types of this disease.

137

The reasons for establishing CNSI. The first reason was that the Wake Forest School of Medicine in Winston-Salem, NC purchased a building downtown in the business district and they needed to fill it. It was decided that the Department of Physiology and Pharmacology would be moved and for 3-4 months the administration lied to us that we were not going to be moved so as to keep the troops in line. I must say that chairs I knew previously were not liars and heavy handed administrators, but as we will see below, I did not learn this lesson immediately. As I was studying Alzheimer's disease at the time, leaving the main medical campus seemed a bit absurd but I was not bringing in enough money to be counted in the inner, decision-making circle so off to the downtown research center I went with most of the rest of the department. We were told to form companies as this would further enrich the school. Eventually most of these faculty members left the school. Being the curmudgeon that I have always been, I set up a non-profit company with my wife. A non-profit company does not have owners and stock but instead works with donations that receive a tax benefit. This meant that the school could not own CNSI and profit from it. No one knew this and apparently did not care enough to look into it; one for our team.

The second reason for forming CNSI is that our research often diverged from the mainstream National Institutes of Health review priorities. In other words, if you proposed research that was too far off the beaten path and had the temerity to suggest innovative research that went beyond their views, as we did in 1991 with our pain research, funding would not be forthcoming. At this time we studied Alzheimer's disease instead because the reviewers could not fathom how cingulate cortex was involved in pain and surprisingly that pain had anything to do with emotion. They said that this cortex has no specific role in pain processing. Our first study published in 1992 showed this to be clearly incorrect. I went to Hammersmith Hospital in London for three months to do human studies to make certain my conclusions were correct (they were) and they have been validated numerous times since in all species analyzed including mice, rats, monkeys and humans. Thus, we needed a method of supporting innovative research during dry periods of support until the research community caught up with what we were doing. The CNSI was this mechanism.

Originally CNSI was meant to be an educational resource for mid-career scientists and to provide consulting services. Each scientist stayed at CNSI for 1 week to three months to amplify their studies of cingulate cortex. We emphasized the structure, brain connections, and functions of the cingulate cortex in relationship to their specific interests. Over the years CNSI has evolved into a more disease oriented undertaking. Indeed, we have now made the mechanisms and treatment of survivors of adolescent abuse our primary focus. See our web site at www.cingulumneurosciences.org for our past and current focus, the latter of which is using an animal model of physical abuse to analyze changes directly in the brain rather than with human imaging from outside of the cranium. In the last vignette these types of studies are discussed in terms of their value to understanding brain and cingulate mechanisms and potential for treatment of abuse survivors.

VIGNETTE 26

First Mental Breakdown

AS IN MOST research-oriented medical schools, a new chairman's arrival at Upstate Medical University was heralded by the president with great fanfare because of all the money Dr. Michael W. Miller brought with him from Tulane University. In contrast, I had a more subdued level of funding but was recruited to his department of neuroscience and physiology for three activities; teach in the neuroscience course, develop NIH funding for my laboratory and help him and a group of alcohol researchers attain a large program project grant (~5 million dollars). I have never been as impressed with money as my colleagues but rather tended to prioritize scientific issues that I thought needed consideration whether or not grant reviewers concurred with me. This had its ups as it kept me focused on my key issues and downs as I often found myself paddling up the money stream rather than down it. My focus was cingulate cortex and its role in pain but not alcohol abuse or alcohol-induced brain damage. I also spent too much time in my laboratory doing research rather than gossiping with colleagues in the hallways and so would miss out on some of the common knowledge that others had. Generally speaking this helped maintain my unique scientific focus and productivity but in one profound instance it was a severe detriment as related here.

In 2011 a departmental meeting was called so that Dr. Miller could "make a statement." It appears that he was stepping down as chair due to scientific fraud. His comments were quite vague as he never agreed

First Mental Breakdown

that he engaged in fraud; sociopaths rarely do. This hit me, but no one else, like a brick wall as I was not in the gossiping loop. What is more, I had allowed my tenure to be used to attract another scientist (an excellent one I might add) so I was at the mercy of the department for support. Here is a copy of parts of the report by James T. Mulder in the Syracuse Post Standard on February 28, 2012.

"Former high-ranking scientist at Upstate Medical faked research, federal investigation shows"

A former Upstate Medical University scientist has been sanctioned for falsifying results of federally-funded research. Michael W. Miller, of Manlius, the former chairman of Upstate's department of neuroscience and physiology, fudged data in four studies funded by the National Institute of Alcohol Abuse and Alcoholism and the National Institutes of Health, according to the federal Office of Research Integrity, which investigates research misconduct.

He also falsified or made up data in two published studies; those were retracted by two scientific journals last month, the federal agency said. The agency published the findings of its investigation on its Web site and in the Federal Register. The agency said Miller altered bar graphs to make experimental results appear valid, fabricated text in a manuscript describing mice experiments and falsified other data to exaggerate the effect alcohol exposure had during fetal development…

The Office of Research Integrity said, "Dr. Miller neither admits nor denies committing research misconduct but accepts ORI has found evidence of research misconduct." The agency said Miller has agreed not to contract or subcontract with any federal agency for one year. After that one year period expires, Miller has agreed to have any research he does supervised for two years. Two scientific journals … retracted two papers co-authored by Miller after Upstate informed the journals its investigation showed the researcher had committed misconduct..."

Comments

Why do I bring up quotes from this article about Miller's fraud case? Because it is an example of the sociopathic personality and it had a direct and serious impact on my psychiatric life. Dr. Miller was physically walked off the campus and I was left with one year to get my whits about me before being removed even though I had nothing to do with his fraud. Although a member of the union and paying dues for a decade, I was told they could do nothing about my sacking. But they really do have an opulent building in Albany, NY for which my dues were used in one way or another. I take you through this because, while I was not enamored with the school after seeing this and a number of other fraudulent activities by the President, Vice President of Finance, and dean (at this point the school seemed to me to be a cesspool), it evoked a full-blown mental breakdown for me; something I had never experienced before. I chose to take a position at Boston University School of Medicine that has an impeccable reputation and qualified individuals at each level of the organization where I am a Research Professor to this day.

Miller is certainly a sociopath by which we mean a dangerous romantic partner, a scammer on the internet, a liar at work, or someone pushing a bogus business deal. Miller has a smooth and often jovial personality. He was easy to get along with and worked well in grant review committees at the NIH. Of course, none of this was apparent from the perspective of his being a sociopath when he hired me to an Upstate job. It is almost impossible to identify the sociopathic personality without observing their behavioral patterns before they emerge. In Miller's case it only became clear after the above reported events; long after anything could be done to stop him.

To see a sociopath in action, watch Jerry Lundegaard (Steve Buscemi), the sales manager of a car dealership in the movie *"Fargo."* He is a smooth talking conman engaged in a financial fraud including collateralizing a large loan with nonexistent cars. For comparison, consider his psychopathic accomplice played by Peter Stormare who kills a cop and two people that saw their crime and goes to the cabin to watch TV; no facial expression, no emotion, no empathy. He later kills his partner with an axe and puts him through a wood chipper.

My removal from Upstate evoked my first mental breakdown (MB#1 on my Lifeline). A mental (nervous) breakdown refers to a state of intense emotional stress that is almost entirely controlled by emotion and associated with increased cardiovascular changes without rational thought and mine is an example. Being fired from one's job is often a cause of severe stress. I screamed out the second floor window of our home that I was going to shoot myself, pulled a banister off the wall in the basement and performed some destructive interior redecorating with it. The police were called and could not settle me down, so I was tased three times in the back and brought to the police station for photographs of my wounds. They were minor; nothing like Stanley used to inflict. I was then taken to the mental health facility for one night. This, however, would not be my last breakdown and encounter with the police and their tasers.

My mental breakdown was not as horrific and dramatic as some, but to me it was quite grave as I was carried out of my home strapped on a gurney, put into an ambulance and admitted to the local mental health clinic. It demonstrated that, while functional, I was operating on the edge of my mental capabilities. Sadly, it was not my last; I had one more to go.

VIGNETTE 27

Second Mental Breakdown

IN LATE 2016 Emily and I had a vigorous argument in which she called me small brained and my wife commented on how little I had accomplished in terms of my last 30 years of self-diagnosis which was not entirely true. Apparently this evoked the attitude that Blanche would take of quiet disdain and overlooking issues that were significant to me. This threw me into a rage that evoked copious amounts of yelling and swearing. As noted in Vignette 4, this is clearly a form of emotional abuse towards Emily and her mother. But I raised the stakes by grabbing her finger and pulling it back. It appears that my mental demons were alive and doing well in my brain contrary to my previous beliefs (MB#2 on my Lifeline). Lukas intervened and we struggled until the police were called.

After the police arrived, three of them were in a standoff with me in the kitchen while I held a knife to my chest and threatened to impale myself. One of the officers apparently had not been counseled in crisis negotiating and yelled, "Go ahead, do it!" Yikes, he was telling a mentally ill stranger to kill himself! I started to put the knife into my chest and told Emily "this is real cutting;" by which I meant suicide. As the blood began to appear on my T-shirt the police fired their three tasers at me which I pulled off my chest thinking I beat them. They started pepper spraying me to which I turned my back and it too had no effect. I was really "winning" this standoff. BUT the wet pepper spray made their tasers more effective as it completed the electrical circuit and on the second taser volley to my back I went down. I was again strapped

Second Mental Breakdown

to a gurney, placed in an ambulance where the attendants took my vital signs and they took me to hospital. After the interns and residents had a brief viewing of my small wound that only took 5 stiches to close, I was placed in a temporary room where I pulled out my intravenous lines and got out of bed to leave in my gown with no shoes. This was in the middle of a Syracuse winter; picture me in this state wandering the streets as I started looking like my homeless "brothers and sisters." The electronic doors were shut to prevent me from leaving and I was given a candy-striper to keep me on suicide watch before being taken back to the mental health facility.

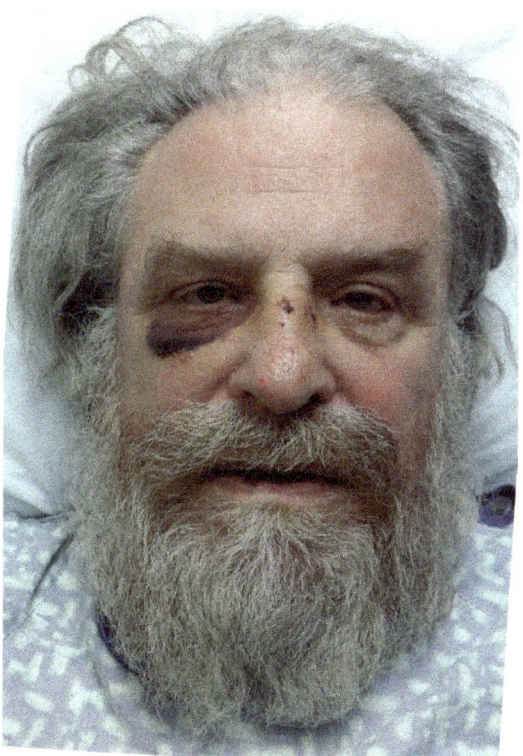

This picture of me in my hospital gown shows my state following this event. The black eye and cut were produced during a fall in the kitchen during the general malay to capture and subdue me. This is an angry and violent man; an abuse survivor with PTSD.

Thus, a few days later I realized that in my mental closet there was a shelf with parental abuse (remember the triple-hit model of parental abuse in Vignette 14) of physical, neglectful and emotional abuse on it. I had realized this before, but never had such a clear demonstration of how much it affected me as an adult. One doesn't want to open my closet as it can precipitate intense anger and rage. Fortunately for me and those with whom I relate, Dialectical Behavioral Therapy and Zoloft appear to have moderated or eliminated such negative behaviors. However, this has taken a toll on my family as both Emily and her mom remain sensitized to it to this day. It appears that no one is more qualified to study the brain alterations produced by adolescent abuse than I am.

VIGNETTE 28

From Intension Tremors to Near Death

I WAS TAKING Depakote (also termed valproate) for bipolar disorder and it effectively blocked my manic/depressive symptoms. As noted earlier, April-May was always a good time in graduate school because that is when I was seasonally manic and got the most work done; i.e., collecting and analyzing data. Symptoms can be used to enhance productivity and insight so use them when you can, don't fight them if possible. That is the good news. However, there was bad news associated with Depakote in combination with Lamotrigine that literally brought me to my knees and near death.

    I was experiencing intension tremors; shaking of the right hand when intending to do something intricate. Although I did not realize it at the time, 6 years earlier my right hand shook so intensely that I spilled coffee from a cup during a conference in Jena, East Germany. I got the cup refilled and the coffee splashed onto the arm of a colleague's sport coat. He was quite generous in excusing me and his empathy was obvious as he was just too excited because this was the first time well- known Western neuroscientists were attending a conference in his part of Germany. What I did not know at the time was that this was the beginning of my intension tremors. A few years passed and they started getting worse (3 years before the following events). In fact, not only did the right hand tremor progress, it started in the left hand and on three occasions my legs started to shake uncontrollably such that I would have to sit down.

I saw a neurologist to determine if these tremors were a prelude to Parkinson's Disease. They noted there were none of the classical signs such as pill rolling with the fingers, lack of spontaneous arm movements when walking or lack of emotional facial expressions. They concluded that the Depakote may have been causing the tremors as this is one of its known side effects. That was also very good news as treatment for Parkinson's Disease was not indicated. In order to remove the Depakote and still have treatment for bipolar disorder, I was placed on an escalating dose of the antiseizure drug Lamotrigine with the goal of removing the Depakote when the former drug was at full dose.

Lamotrigine is an antiseizure medication used alone or in combination with other antiseizure medications and common side effects include *dizziness, shaking (tremors), loss of coordination and drowsiness among others*. I highlight these four as they were the ones that were relevant to my condition. In order to wean me off Depakote/valproate, they scaled me into Lamotrigine that would be followed by a slow withdrawal of Depakote so my bipolar disorder would not present problems. Things did not go according to plan. During this month the tremors did indeed stop; but…

On New Year's Eve December 31, 2018, at the highest dose of Lamotrigine and still receiving the full dose of Depakote, it was noticed by my son and wife that I was getting weaker on stressful tasks such as moving a treadmill from one floor to the next. That evening my feet were swollen, I was breathing heavily and leaning to the left. I got tired early and went to bed. At 2 AM I fell in the bathroom and had trouble getting up without help and appeared confused. After being put in bed and about every hour thereafter I tried to get up to urinate with the same result and could walk but unsteadily. I was told not to go downstairs without help; however, for some unknown reason, I did try to go downstairs and fell down a flight of oak stairs onto a marble floor. No bones were broken; why not? I had learned when working on a ladder outside that if I was going to fall, it was best to simply allow the fall to happen without reaching out with my arms to break the fall but rather roll with the fall and I never broke bones. When teaching snowboarding, my son begins with teaching his students how to fall. It may have been that I used this strategy unconsciously during the fall down the stairs or delirium was setting in and I had no perception of falling.

I was found with my legs tangled, could not get up and it appeared I was delirious. My wife, son and daughter picked me up dazed and sat me in a chair while being dressed. At this point I was driven to the emergency room and taken to the Medical Surgery Unit with very weak and labored breathing. A whole body imaging scan was negative and I was evaluated by neurology and internal medicine. As the scan came back negative (fortunately I was not having a stroke), it was determined that I had congestive heart failure as my lungs were filling with fluid. I was started on Lasix to clear this fluid. My mental status declined as I could not tell the nurses the month when asked or where I was. When asked who they were pointing to, I said it was my beautiful wife. As this was the only correct answer, I got many points from Leslie. That was a good thing as she spoon fed me for the next three days. I used the urinal and one time said I was done but was not and sprayed all over her. I could not turn over in bed. The delirium increased and I started cycling into fevers and kept trying to bite the finger monitor off. When asked why, I simply responded, "I don't know." On the second day I had to wear mittens on both hands because I pulled my I.V.s out. I could not eat alone on the second day and a more detailed brain imaging did not show stroke or other issues, although an old lesion possibly due to Blanche's hitting my head was observed. My heart and lungs were responding well after the regime of Lasix. I do not remember the first 4 days of the hospital stay due to my delirium and the above comments were relayed to me by Leslie.

I could not get out of bed but became cognizant of my surroundings and the time and the delirium started to clear. I was still barely speaking and living in a diaper with serious fever that brought the "SWAT" team as the situation was so grave. This team is comprised of emergency medical staff in case I coded. Death was not far away, but, in my delirium, I did not know this. On the next day I was looking better and they wanted to do a lumbar puncture to see if white blood cells were in the fluid surrounding the spinal cord that would indicate an infection. As I was on Xarelto; a blood thinner to prevent clotting and stroke, the lumbar puncture had to wait until I was taken off Xarelto for a long enough time for it to clear from my system so it would not enhance bleeding from the procedure. At this time I was seen by the infectious disease, toxicology and rheumatology groups. They did not have the slightest idea what was going on. I was tested for Lyme disease, encephalitis and a number of other diseases; all of which came back negative. I was put on three antibiotics, one antiviral and a steroid. Further imaging with something called a contrast agent showed nothing more of consequence and the delirium was clearing. I watched movies, got up for rehabilitation and an electroencephalogram (electo-head-graph) was performed and all came back normal. I find the latter observation surprising given my extensive history with psychiatric maladies. It should not have been normal.

A week after admission, I was getting weaker and was put on oxygen, running a high fever and the SWAT team was called in again. Another brain scan was negative as was the lumber puncture; most cycling fevers occurred overnight but the lumbar puncture showed no signs of infection (no white blood cells). At this point it was concluded that the Lamotrigine was the likely culprit and it was removed along with the Depakote. As I was no longer delirious, I was placed in the Rehabilitation Department for physical, speech and occupational therapy. It was concluded that I had an encephalopathy as my brain may have temporarily swelled.

After complete removal of Depakote for a few days, I was put on half dose when it was restarted; at half dose the intention tremors resolved as demonstrated by the fact that much of this text was written 2-9 months later using the computer mouse and keypad. Sleep was encouraged with low dose melatonin which enhanced going to sleep but did not keep me sleeping through the entire night. After three weeks of physical therapy, I was sent home to live entirely on the first floor; I was not allowed to use stairs due to the risk of falling. On the first floor,

I showered, slept, eat and worked.

Summary and Suggestions. If I did not have bipolar disorder (BD) that required Depakote/valproate treatment, the events relayed here would not have been an issue. The combination of it with Lamotrigine (two antiseizure medications) was deadly to me. Although this experience brought me close to death, no infections were found to explain spiking night fever, three antibiotics and one antiviral were administered and a lumbar puncture was clear; i.e., no blood cells were in the fluid surrounding the brain to suggest an infection. No central nervous system problems such as stroke or vascular problems could be detected with computed tomography or magnetic resonance imaging. Given the side effects of Lamotrigine, the severe fall and subsequent delirium associated with the encephalopathy following it were likely due to Lamotrigine alone or in combination with Depakote. At half dose of Depakote, the intension tremors ceased, there were no further falling episodes or delirium and the BD was and is well controlled. This experience alerts to the fact that drug side effects may at times be as or more important than the direct positive effects. Although multiple anti-seizure drugs can be used, in my case this was contraindicated.

VIGNETTE
29

Classical Conditioning, the Placebo Effect and Abuse

MULTIPLE ABUSE EVENTS of the same type or multiple forms given as discipline or for the pleasure of the predator evoke changes in the brain that are much more harmful than single events. One of the likely reasons for this is that repeated abuse acquires a life of its own through a process called classical conditioning. You might recall my sister's autonomic reactions of shaking when on telephone calls with Blanche. They did not stop until the conversation was concluded. The context and other person would evoke them through a process called classical conditioning.

Classical conditioning is a learning process, first observed by Ivan Pavlov in the 1890s who was studying salivation with dogs. He found that providing a dog food would trigger salivation just like we experience when the cook is busy in the kitchen preparing a meal. If Pavlov rang a bell each time he fed the dog, at some point he could ring the bell (the conditional stimulus) and that alone would evoke salivation without giving it a meal (the unconditional stimulus). Of course, one can extinguish this response by frequently not pairing the stimuli; i.e., the meal and bell. In other words the previously neutral stimulus (bell) acquired the psychological meaning of a motivationally meaningful stimulus (food) and salivation was Pavlov's objective measure of the response.

Modern neuroscience has explored the mechanisms of what is termed the placebo effect which is another form of classical conditioning.

Classical Conditioning, the Placebo Effect and Abuse

This occurs, for example, when a patient is given a powerful pain killer under identifiable conditions including the color of a pill or cream and administration by a medical doctor who provides specific instructions about its use and effects. After a number of trials, one can switch the active drug for an inactive compound (a sugar pill or cream) and, as long as all other conditions are kept the same including the doctor and his/her instructions, the patient will continue to experience pain relief. Two issues are of particular note. First, it is the patient's belief that the doctor's instructions are correct to establishing this effect. However, multiple presentations of the placebo will eventually result in losing its pain relieving effect just as the bell did for Pavlov's dogs. Second, both of these forms of classical conditioning establish a series of events in the brain that predict outcomes based on previous experience. In other words, they are learning experiences that are in fact automatic. Joe Dispenza provides an excellent account of the similarities between classical conditioning and the placebo effect in a presentation titled "Pavlov's Dogs and the Placebo Effect" (November 2, 2015; the World Summit of Integrative Medicine, entitled "Healing by Thought Alone;" http://worldsummitintegrativemedicine).

Why is this learning perspective relevant to abuse in one or more of its forms? Children and adolescents quickly learn the context of their abuse and the perpetrator and anticipate it whether or not the experience is present or forthcoming. If a male predator, for example, has raped a girl, she will automatically respond to him the same way even if he is not going to revictimize her. I certainly was conditioned to harsh physical abuse by being beaten by Stanley. When Blanche said, "I am going to tell your father about this when he gets home and you will be punished," I immediately ran to my bedroom and started crying because I had been conditioned to such abuse. He actually did not have to beat me after multiple beatings because the damage had already been done to my brain. In another example, playing my coronet in church would set off a stress response and the context of a church service itself would be stressful. Also as noted above, my sister was so traumatized by Blanche that she would shake during telephone calls. While the fight-or-flight stress response is an important coping feature of our lives, abuse conditioning produces dysfunctional stress and what is termed psychogenic pain (pain generated in the psyche).

Conclusions. It appears to take child and adolescent survivors of abuse a decade or more to recognize the impact of abuse on them. One reason for the long delay in their awareness is due to the time it takes to extinguish their responses due to mechanisms of classical conditioning in the brain. Another reason is their shame and efforts to dissociate themselves from such events. When they finally do so, anger emerges from them and they call for retribution as observed in the Catholic priest, child abuse scandal. Abusive parents are conditioning their children and further alienating them. The survivors are the only ones that can remediate their situations, particularly if they are adult survivors of adolescent abuse.

VIGNETTE
30

"True" Belief & Free Will versus Genes & Environment

"I have no theories to uphold, no prejudices to subserve, no interests to advance, no instructions to fulfill; I am a free agent."
Journalist William H. Russell (1863)

As a neuroscientist I must restate this,
"If not for my genes, brain and adolescence; I would be a free agent. These are guardrails to my free agency."

IN OTHER WORDS, while I think I have "free will" (choice), there are many circumstances that militate against its being completely free. This vignette is about the extent to which we have what philosophers and scientists alike refer to as "free will." This issue is raised here for three reasons. First, my presumed ADHD genes predispose me and some of you to particular behaviors over which we have little volitional control, second because my parents tried to set the physical conditions for a Fundamentalist life through Bible readings and church, and third, because of their abuse to engender the latter. ADHD and child and adolescent abuse appears to formulate the conditions under which vulnerable survivors must live often for their entire lives and it can interfere with their free will.

Where did the concept of free will arise? Although neuroscientists debate the brain substrates of free will, they generally couch it in very short term events (seconds-minutes-hours). On the grander scale of where the concept arose, it appears to have been generated in a religious context as it was a necessity when "God" created man and woman as reported in Biblical teachings. Whether or not he/she did is not the issue. The notion arose as he/she did not want to create a population of automatons but wanted them to have the free will needed to request salvation; therefore we have a choice to accept or reject him/her. Thus, one sets in motion this debate on a large scale. One could argue that of course I have the freedom or not to accept Christ. I would argue that my ADHD genes and as an abuse survivor from religious zealots, I do not have a "totally free" choice but might instead, out of anger, reject him/her. The same issue arises with gays and lesbians. Do they have a freedom of choice? I would argue that their genetics establishes the basis for their lives and it has little to do with free will or choice. Trying to pray away biology, as in the Pray Away the Gay movement, is doomed from the start just as it is with Catholic priest celibacy; both are antithetical approaches to biology in trying to repress basic biological instincts.

Free will or volition is the mental (brain) function whereby we initiate, maintain, or actively discontinue a behavior; in particular one performed in opposition to pain, discomfort, fatigue, distraction, emotions, or external impediments. There are brain diseases that interrupt an individual's free will/volition including Tourette's syndrome and obsessive-compulsive disorder. Most of us are aware of corprolelia in the former disease that is associated with blurting out spontaneous and inappropriate swearing, yelling, behavioral tics, etc. that are not volitional and actually embarrassing to the patient. The sense of being out of control or of relinquishing control to an urge can be a source of distress and they often feel guilt for these behaviors. Treatment can fully restore their voluntary control over these behaviors to greatly improve their life. Thus, there are examples of diseases where free will is lost due to the brain's malfunctioning. Late stage Alzheimer's disease tragically removes free will and many other brain functions. Biblical teachings are remarkably silent about these issues as it was written at a time when followers were truly ignorant of scientific realities. It is time to put this book in the dustbin of history and reject its ill-conceived and biologically irrelevant viewpoints.

Due to free will we routinely persevere for long periods of time in our intensions, overcoming all kinds of obstacles. Free will seems to exist as a practical matter in healthy individuals but genetics and abuse can interfere with it. What abusive parents are doing for their own predatory goals is trying to subvert the adolescent's will.

The will, therefore, is a non-reflex part of behavior, it enhances the direction of actions and thought including resistance against sudden changes in mental actions and, like an emotion, the will supports actions and the direction of thought. The will is influenced by long-term events, i.e., not just by events occurring immediately in time, but also by remote history and bears a relationship to the complex emotions of guilt, regret where we feel guilty about bad things we've willfully done, we regret good things that we willfully did not do, and we feel proud about good things that we willfully did. Finally, the will directs us in persisting with aversive behaviors; it helps do the harder thing. My studying cingulate cortex for almost 50 years is an example of persistent free will. So I cannot argue that there is no free will even for genetically disrupted and abused survivors. The will, however, has *guard rails that limit choice.*

Like the will, each of the emotions can direct attention and behavior. For example, one may clench a fist in anger, flee in horror, turn away in disgust, and leap for happiness. These are behaviors where attention is rapidly diverted. There is a close link between emotion and motor function. Indeed, the very word "e-motion" means something out of which motion comes. Thus, a way to conceive of the "will" is as emotions with primary emotions being anger, disgust, fear, happiness, sadness, and surprise.

Stanley used to ask me, "What will you give people if not Jesus?" As a budding humanist studying undergraduate philosophy, I thought that an honest sense of self would be adequate and a well-conceived notion of morality and ethics but that never seemed enough for him because he was seriously worried about Hell and damnation not personal development. He did not realize the strict Biblical box he was living in and could not get out of; he was not a free thinker and did not have a completely free will.

The Normal Son: Free to Choose? The politically conservative Christian Fundamentalist cult views Biblical teachings as the actual word of God given through various prophets, disciples and teachers. The word of God applies as written and only diverges if absolutely necessary from a stated doctrine. When all logic, facts and rationality fail, God fills in the cracks with his "infinite wisdom." The free agency is paramount for someone to "accept Jesus into their heart," one must be free to choose Jesus or Lucifer. One might quibble over why anyone would actually choose the devil and Hell's damnation, but that is for another time.

My parents had a clear conundrum. Their first born was a wayward son in their view. No matter how much they beat him, baptized him, enrolled him in Sunday school and summer Christian Bible camps and sent him to bible school to prepare for the ministry, he just did not seem to bow to "God's will"; as per their interpretation of the Holy Scriptures. What was their solution to this conundrum, particularly as things were not going so well with my sister? The answer is the answer that most religious cults employ; an isolated society with options limited to adolescents to choices that are acceptable to the Christian community; i.e., Blanche's and Stanley's view of isolation meaning that we are in the world but not of it. As this is a form of neglect, one can view many strict fundamentalist cults (not only Christian) as abusive.

The question now arises; did my brother (the good son because he chose the religious path of salvation and a life bathed in the blood of Christ) have a choice in his life? His parents learned that beating their children did not produce the expected outcomes and made family interactions worse, although their insights into family dynamics were virtually non-existent. Maybe Brian was normal but he also was not abused. In fact, the level of abuse was promulgated in the Vogt family according to birth order; Brent receiving the most vigorous abuse,

"True" Belief & Free Will versus Genes & Environment

Betsy receiving less and Brian receiving none.

What did Brian learn? Did his children have free will to choose in their lives? It appears the Southern Fundamentalist Christians believe that the key to good religious parenting is limiting the range of options available except when you do not agree with them. For example, thou shalt not kill is a commandment. To the religious, this actually means thou shalt not kill unless, for example, you want to stop the spread of Communism in Vietnam or establish a Mideast outpost in Iraq and a plethora of other justifications for killing. So the commandment to not kill is not absolute; it is flexible based on circumstances. Biblical scholars guide the confused supplicant through this maze of contradictions to a harmonious conclusion with lots of cement based on the wishes of "God" that we often do not understand but must just believe.

The movie "The Truman Show" directed by Peter Weir with Jim Carrey playing Truman highlights the fundamentalist approach to child rearing. Truman doesn't know it, but everything in his life is part of a massive TV set. Executive producer Christof orchestrates "The Truman Show" in a live broadcast of Truman's every move captured by hidden cameras. Christof tries to control Truman's mind, even removing his true love, Sylvia from the show and replacing her with Meryl. As Truman gradually discovers the truth, however, he must decide whether or not to act on it. This is the Bob Jones University approach to education and child rearing. Devise a completely fabricated environment to assure that from birth to death all participants play the same tune as in a grand orchestra. At this school there are well controlled environments from infant to undergraduate education. By limiting options and the environmental context to the Biblical path, they help guarantee that their children will make the "right" choices when it comes to living a good Christian life including one of seeking salvation. Were my brother's children free to choose Christ in this context? No. They did not as they were living a form of "The Truman Show."

Provide a completely controlled environment in which options are minimal and a child will believe and follow the prescribed religious views and principles often into adulthood. This applies to all fundamentalist religious extremists as well; not just the "Fundies" in South Carolina. If this controlled environment is maintained throughout adolescence, the probability of a child leaving the fold is greatly diminished as their lives are built on such principles and no other options are entertained. At the end of the film, Truman takes the improbable path and leaves the great geosphere that was his home for more than two decades. His acquaintances and family relations were all contrived and his beliefs proved to be flawed; he had to have a serious transition period in his life. It appears to me that most of the human population lives in various contrived worlds with the local religious beliefs passed on from one generation to the next. I certainly felt like Truman when making the early transition in my 20s and leaving the Christian Geosphere to create a new person and over-ride some of the consequences of parental abuse.

How do we resolve the conundrum of free will in the context of genes and environment (abuse)? ADHD genes are to some extent deterministic as are the outcomes produced by abusive parents and predators. Nevertheless, I made choices that contradicted my upbringing. We must conclude that, while there is no "universal free will" that allows us to make any choice; we live in a biological context that provides barriers to our unlimited freedom. Thus, "free will" is only partially "free."

The long-term vision of curing brain diseases: The Pearly Gates. The Pearly Gates referred to in Christian religions refer to a time after death when the "spirit" (quotes required because there is no scientific evidence for such an entity) is presumed to go to "Heaven" (another mythical place) and where "Saint Paul" will meet all those that have been cleansed by the saving grace and blood of Jesus. Well, that sounds a bit fanciful to an atheist, but that does not mean we live free of goals and in a new reality.

I propose that in the framework of this book, the Pearly Gates are found, for example, at the exit to our penal systems where convicts including criminal psychopaths are greeted by neuroscientists rather than Saint Paul; a time when the products of abuse have been cured in as many as 40% of prison inmates. The neuroscience atheists will greet the inmates as they leave prison and wish them well as they have been cured of their disease(s) with which they suffered. This is my dream.

Summary and Suggestions. I often say that my brain provides me with a rich resource (cesspool) of psychiatric disease that gives me unique insights into how the brain functions and dysfunctions. It provides me with scientific challenges that healthy individuals can only observe from a distance without realizing the importance of links between genes, adolescence, and brain-abused impairments in behavior. My brain cesspool and a life challenge to understand it has led me on a unique path as, had I killed my parents, as I often fantasized during my middle adolescence, I would have followed another path often followed by my "brothers and sisters"; a life of crime and punishment. Jails are full to bursting with individuals with serious brain diseases needing treatment rather than punishment.

The question addressed in this vignette is whether or not we have free will and my conclusion is yes, to a point. That is to say that there are guard rails that limit choice. These guard rails include 1) the strict fundamentalist approach of limiting children's experiences so they do not diverge from the rules of salvation and a prescribed life style. 2) Genetic composition that regulate behaviors as in ADHD. 3) Child and adolescent abuse that evoke anxiety, PTSD and other psychopathologies. 4) Environmental factors such as low socioeconomic status in low income intra-city neighborhoods that can engender youth violence. 5) The ravages of aging as expressed in Alzheimer's and Parkinson's Diseases. Thus, free will is only free to a point.

While we incarcerate psychopaths for violent crimes, this should only be done until we can find biologically-based solutions for their brain diseases. This is one of the major challenges of the biomedical sciences.

Finally, parents with one or more children with ADHD have seen many examples of odd or outrageous behaviors similar to mine including impaired driving habits in late adolescence that simply do not fit the world view of healthy and even abusive parents. However, we argued here that the behavior of children with ADHD is due to genes that have social, cognitive and evolutionary value, not just deficiencies. With particular effort, including parental or close-companion guidance and drug therapy, they can employ their own unique capabilities and become quite successful in adult undertakings. Abusive punishment will not change this fact. Thus, even cognitively and socially impaired individuals have some ability to express free will.

VIGNETTE
31

What is Suffering?

VIGNETTE 4 STATES that vulnerable survivors of harsh abuse suffer with various psychopathologies including anxiety and panic disorders, PTSD, depression and chronic pain syndromes all of which can result in substance use disorder even as adults as a form of self-medication. The latter involves alcoholism and illicit (non-prescription) opioid misuse which can result in severe dependence and often death. Knowing this, one must wonder why survivors engage in such behaviors. It seems obvious they are trying to alleviate their suffering. But what is suffering and how can it be alleviated without engaging in drug abuse?

While having dinner with a colleague in Dusseldorf, Germany, a woman and her husband in an adjacent booth asked if they could interrupt for a moment and tell us about her chronic pain. She related that every morning before getting out of bed, she had to rehearse what she would be doing. As every movement evoked pain, she could not simply go about her day as the typical individual. In other words, she constantly suffered with her chronic pain associated with joint or muscle movement. Chronic pain affects more people than cardiovascular disease, cancer, and diabetes combined. Like many Americans, I have a moderate low back pain that may become chronic. I adopt the same strategy as this woman but on a more limited scale. When doing heavy work outside such as moving 8 cubic yards of top soil or cementing and laying tons of brickwork and mortar, I am careful to move slowly, with minimal rotation and bending. When I do bend, I stay in that position for as long as possible so as not to damage my back further. I take frequent brakes laying flat on my back to give it a time out. One must "listen" to what their pain system is saying. At the end of the day, I take a very hot bath to relax my back muscles. Curing chronic pain is one of the many challenges of pain research that has not yet been resolved, although we can block it with powerful opioids. The question arises from these patients and abuse survivors is; what is suffering?

Suffering appears to be an inability to escape the source of pain and stress. Not all pain is generated by peripheral nerves in body tissues (skin, muscle, joints, and intestines). Some can be generated in the psyche (psycho-genic pain); the brain is quite adept at developing its own reality. Here are three examples that all are documented to influence aMCC and may be considered for pain, stress and abuse therapies, although I personally have not employed them. 1) The placebo effect discussed above involves administering an inactive drug but all the conditions including statements by the physician support the notion that one is getting an active, pain-relieving drug. The placebo effect convinces you that you have received the active drug and you feel better even though you have received a "sugar" pill. 2) Hypnosis is another example in which the conditions set by the hypnotist can be used to induce a state even for the relief of pain during major surgeries such as mastectomy. (Google Marie-Elisabeth Faymonville who has performed thousands of major surgeries under hypnosis instead of general anesthesia.) Finally, meditation, particularly focused attention using rhythmic breathing while disengaging from external or internal thoughts and stimuli has been shown to have an organic basis in the brain (e.g., Fox and colleagues, *Neuroscience and Biobehavioral Reviews*, volume 65, pages 208-228). Experienced individuals at mindfulness of breathing show improvement in pACC function that is not observed in non-meditators (Hölzel and colleagues, 2007; *Neuroscience Letters*, volume 421, pages 16-21). However, while this approach has been used to relieve pain and stress, it has not been studied with abuse survivors. Moreover, imaging findings in this field are still quite variable and the effective parameters are not yet well established.

The underlying mechanism of all of these approaches is the ability to control to some extent our emotional responses. A very interesting study was performed in 2004 (Salomons and colleagues, *Journal of Neuroscience*, volume 24 issue 24, pages 7199-7203) in which healthy subjects were told that they could control the amount of heat pain they would receive on the back of their hand by moving a joystick. There were two conditions, one in which they had control of the thermal stimulation and one in which they did not. In the latter instance, however, they were not told that they actually did not have control of the temperature as it was held constant under this condition. Ironically, the imaging signals were *reduced* in part of cingulate cortex as one would expect during pain relief. When the pain signal was not controllable, the cingulate signal was elevated as in a normal pain response (Vignette 2). Thus, it is the controllability of the pain signal that is of particular importance to the psychogenic aspects of pain and stress. You need to believe you have control and this can modulate your brain responses and relieve suffering to some extent. This is true for the placebo effect, hypnoanalgesia and meditation. The most effective medications are opioids such as hydrocodone and oxycodone, the former of which I rarely use when the pain reaches 8 on a scale of 0-10. These drugs are highly addictive and must be used sparingly.

This is not to say that all pain is psychogenic and can be willfully controlled. There are many conditions such as fibromyalgia, temporomandibular joint disorder, spinal compression injuries and pelvic muscle pain that are not easily controlled and may be impervious to such efforts. Indeed, most forms of chronic pain may fit this class of disorders.

Summary and suggestions. Pain is not completely generated by peripheral tissue nerves and can be controlled to some extent by mental interventions. Determining if you have such a manageable type of pain and/or stress is critical as is "listening" to what your body is telling you about the pain and stress signals and taking care to manage them. Suffering, however, is a broader problem of not being able to control any form of pain and/or stress such as the damage evoked by child abuse that often lasts well into adulthood in individuals that are vulnerable to such maltreatments and can evolve into PTSD. Psychiatric insights, meditation, relaxation therapy and hypnosis may help one evolve coping strategies but we have yet to identify a cure for suffering associated with abuse and related syndromes in adolescents and adults.

VIGNETTE 32

The Cycle of Violence

THE CYCLE OF Violence is a well-documented theory that child and adolescent violence is passed on by survivors from their generation to the next in a vicious cycle. I mentioned it earlier in terms of Stanley's upbringing in the Bronx where he was neglected and lived in a violent neighborhood but he did not understand abuse in any of its forms. Previous or current violence in a family is almost never an open topic of conversation but I have known people who were raped during their adolescence and turned into abusers themselves. The Cycle of Violence theory of abuse posits that childhood abuse increases the odds of future delinquency and adult criminality overall by 40% (see Cathy Spatz Widom, 1992; "The Cycle of Violence," National Institute of Justice). This is a crucial subject for abuse survivors to understand.

Let us begin with the Ike and Tina Turner family as there are so many books, movies, commentaries and witnesses to their struggles. Here I summarize this family's experiences as a prelude to understanding my own issues with the Cycle of Violence. I love the robust nature of Tina's voice and her incredible dancing and showomanship. While watching the movie *"What's Love Got to do with It"* on their relationship, I had to stop watching as Ike's vicious beatings increased. It was apparent that there may have been more to the story than was in the movie. Indeed there was. I considered Ike Turner's book with Nigel Cawthorne *"Takin' Back My Name"* (Virgin Books, U.K., 1999) to determine the level of his adolescent abuse; i.e., what he brought to the marriage. The title itself suggests that Ike is about to defend his life without actually understanding it but I was looking for regret about how he treated Tina. As expected, the book moves mostly from one event in his musical career to another; his money issues, his many wives (~12) and his constant sex as an adolescent and adult without insight into his psychosocial experiences and links between sex and personal relationships. I did find evidence of serious adolescent physical and emotional abuse and there is little doubt that Ike was a predator himself both as an adolescent and adult.

Ike was born in Mississippi in 1931 and experienced the worst of the Jim Crow era. Jim Crow laws enforced racial segregation in the South between 1887 and the beginning of the civil rights movement in the 1950s. Jim Crow is the name of a minstrel routine performed beginning in 1828 and the term became a derogatory epithet for African Americans and a designation for their segregated life. Witnessing racial violence by the Ku Klux Klan and other segregationists as an adolescent likely contributed to Ike's adult rage, violence and self-medication with cocaine. While older women took advantage of him sexually, they did it over periods of months and he reports that after a few weeks he began to enjoy it. This may have contributed to his hyper-sexuality rather than abuse *per se*. His father was savagely beaten for having an affair with a white woman and later died from his injuries. Although Ike did not witness it, it caused a serious disruption of his family life and introduced an abusive stepfather.

Ike was beaten for various reasons with weeping willow switches. In one instance his stepfather gave him another whipping but Ike snuck up behind him and hit him on the head with a piece of timber. At one point his stepfather caught him fondling the vagina of a local girl and was beaten with a piece of barbed wire. When in late high school, he saw a black man have his throat cut and his penis and testicles cut off and put in his mouth while unconscious. It is clear that Ike suffered personal, family and social abuse and the Southern segregationists were likely the beginning of the Cycle of Violence in the Turner family.

Ike's book details his gambling, willingness to use a gun that he usually carried, engage in fighting around their concerts as when he

The Cycle of Violence

was an adolescent and later cocaine use. He does "regret" buying cocaine and distributing it to his band (a rare moment of regret). He said that having sex with Tina was "more of a duty and he felt that she was resentful and did not want him to touch her." He apparently did not have any insight into Tina's struggles with him and the effects his abuse had on her and his family (he seriously lacked empathy and likely had a severely disrupted cingulate cortex). He claims Tina and he broke up over his cocaine use; that is only partly true as it did have an effect. Ike did not have the emotional insight into his marriage and family to understand the fundamental and corrosive issues of his abuse. His abuse had a more profound effect on his family than cocaine. When he was "coked" up for 6 days at a time, he was irritable and edgy and had a quicker temper. To Ike, Tina's suicide attempts with sleeping pills were a matter of cowardice. Ike said, "It wasn't that I was insensitive, I was just living too fast even to think about her feelings." He looks back at all his wildness with a "tinge" of regret. "Sure I slapped Tina. We had fights. But I never beat her without thinking." These episodes frequently evoked bleeding. He would fall into a stupor from cocaine in the recording studio and then stay there for weeks at a time. The children were devastated when Ike and Tina boke up but he was unaware of how neglect of his children, showing them his violence and lack of paternal duties influenced his family.

Tina wrote of Ike in her book, *"Love Story,"* "Our life together was defined by abuse and fear, for me, though, sex with Ike had become an expression of hostility - a kind of rape - especially when it began or ended with a beating. What had been ugly and hateful between us before became worse with every snort of cocaine. He threw hot coffee in my face, giving me third-degree burns. He used my nose as a punching bag so many times that I could taste blood running down my throat when I sang. He broke my jaw. And I couldn't remember what it was like not to have a black eye." Ike's cocaine use was likely an effort at self-medication and he died from an overdose in 2007 at age 76. Finally, his oldest son Craig, who saw much of the abuse of his mother, committed suicide when he was just 59. Here we have a clear example of the Cycle of Violence that began with how segregationists treated him and others. It certainly amplified Ike's psychiatric issues that can end in substance abuse disorder and suicide but also can continue into future generations as violence.

A story appeared in *Spin Magazine* written by Edward Kiersh (2015; updated in 2017) titled *"Ike Turner: Why I Beat Tina."* This article shows how Ike's adolescent abuse was turned to Tina and his family and how unaware he was of its effects. Indeed, he thought his violence was normal. "Yeah, I hit her, but I didn't hit her more than the average guy beats his wife. The truth is, our life was no different from the guy next door." Exhausted by these assaults, Ike's promiscuity, and his mounting use of cocaine, Tina tried to commit suicide by taking an overdose of sleeping pills.... He said, "Hey, Bo, you coward, you chickens—t, if you want to kick the bucket, why didn't you jump off an overpass." Then there is an amazing quote, *"I still don't know why she left me. I guess she just didn't want to be named Turner anymore."* Really? That was the problem? I think not.

Thus we have an example of the beginning of the Cycle of Violence by violent segregationists in the South that was transmitted to Ike. The violence and the intense abuse of Ike in his adolescence was transferred to Tina and neglect of his family, who he frequently showed his rage to with extreme consequences. Besides his adopted son Craig's suicide, whether or not his violence will translate into any of his other children awaits the next book on the subject.

My abuse as it relates to the Cycle of Violence. The Cycle of Violence in the Vogt family began with Stanley's upbringing in the Bronx by a dysfunctional family and likely a violent, low socioeconomic immigrant neighborhood. He was an easy target for Blanche's instructions to beat his children. I had hoped that I could avoid entering the Cycle of Violence, although I did not understand it as such during most of my life. Unfortunately it appears that I have only modified it from the harsh physical abuse employed by my parents to mainly emotional abuse. Indeed, even my own violence still occasionally surfaced in my adult years, although it was not turned to my children except in one case as noted in the Second Mental Breakdown. On a trip to the North Carolina shore one evening before my citalopram treatment, I was driving the family and someone cut us off almost hitting our car. This I viewed as an instantaneous challenge that no Boston driver with ADHD could overlook. The accelerator was applied, we caught up to that driver with my wife pleading to stop and let it go. "Sorry babes, that is not a possibility." Pulling up next to him, I slowly drove him off the road and onto the gravel embankment. This was done just enough and with a terrorized family to assure that the other driver would realize it was their lucky day that they would be allowed to enjoy the North Carolina beaches. There are many other examples of such tactical driving but the point here is that it is a form of emotional abuse of the entire family.

Since I personally defined abuse as physical abuse given my background of such abuse, I was unaware of emotional abuse; how it is defined and expressed in a family context. While it is apparent to a healthy normal, it was not to me. I did not appreciate Blanche's neglect as abuse, although I do now in retrospect. Most of my personal emotional abuse was due to intense anxiety during periods of stress. I previously relayed examples of such abuse and stress during coronet playing in church and my mental breakdowns. There were two early incidences during the first 15 years of my second marriage that were enhanced by excess drinking in which anxiety over our finances triggered me to throw a lamp at Leslie to produce a bruise. In another incident, I burned many of the Christmas presents and became angry about a truly minor issue and grabbed her by the neck to get her to be quiet as we had guests in the house and in the process I bruised her. In less violent confrontations with spending, I threatened to destroy the car with a sledge hammer if any new credit cards were opened. I broke a coffee table, television and some fossils from Montana. In these instances I referred to them as "just stuff" "I didn't hit you." Sadly, I was rationalizing my abuse just as Ike Turner had, although on a much more modest scale. It is difficult to draw the line between emotional abuse and violence that I brought from my adolescence, particularly when it is amplified by too much alcohol. There was some verbal abuse to my wife such as when I told her she was stupid and had no insight into things; putting her down. She was blamed for many things and said, "she should not say certain things that would set me off." She said that it was like I had to walk on egg shells and that she was afraid of me because she was not certain what would set me off. I had not broken the Cycle of Violence. Sadly I only shifted it from physical to mostly emotional abuse.

I often had shouting outbursts when the kids would squabble. At one time when driving on a Canadian interstate, they sent me over the edge and I actually stopped in the middle of traffic until they stopped fighting. Property taxes in New York are excessive but we could handle them while I had a job, but one year they were particularly ominous to me and I hit the car dash board on the passenger's side so hard that it bent. Lukas suffered the least from my outbursts, although he witnessed them. There are no other examples of direct confrontation with him. That is the good news; however, Emily did not fare as well.

Verbal abuse as defined in Vignette 4 was the major mode of her abuse. I would call her names such as "pussy" when she was not willing or able to perform a task such as getting a driver's license. This clearly upset her and Leslie told me to find another word. During my second mental breakdown I told Emily, who had been cutting, that this is real cutting, by which I meant actual suicide with a knife. This too had an extremely negative impact on her. I cannot remember all the times and forms of verbal abuse that I put Emily through. However, our successful Dialectical Behavioral Therapy together (Vignette 21) helped but I am afraid that this treatment will live in her brain for some time.

Summary and Suggestions. I used the violent Southern segregationists and the Turner family as a well-known example for considering the Cycle of Violence. I have great respect for Tina Turner, what she went through and for her sharing it with us all. Sadly, if we broaden the definition of abuse, I can see some parallels in my life to that of Ike's. I didn't use guns, engage in frequent sex and fighting or cocaine use, but I did over use alcohol which is now essentially out of my diet and replaced with sparkling water. We both suffered from physical abuse while, for me it also included neglect and him more of verbal abuse. My goal in the family was to avoid harsh physical abuse and raise a family that was relatively normal. Essentially I did that, but my definition of abuse was too restricted to that which I received in the context of ADHD and Fundamentalist Christianity. Thus, I have not been able to completely remove myself from the Cycle of Violence that started with Stanley in the Bronx.

It has been difficult for me to remove myself from engaging in emotional abuse; however, it appears that I have had it under control over the last 5 years and I have great expectations for the next 20 or so years. I can only hope that survivors can eject themselves from the Cycle of Violence with the definition of abuse in the broader perspective provided in Vignette 4; i.e., not limited to the details of their own childhood and adolescent experiences. Passing any form of abuse to adolescents of the next generation will only enhance the violence in our society.

VIGNETTE
33

Can Animal Research Help Understand & Cure Abuse Survivors?

EVOLUTION IS A slow process that occurs over centuries and millennia. It is also conservative by preserving body systems that are needed, while removing those that are not best to adapt a species to its environment. Thus, non-human animals share many of our body and brain systems and can provide insights into ourselves. We have already suggested that an aggressive mouse substrain may help to identify genes associated with violence, aggression and conduct disorder in humans. These same genes may predispose humans to engage in physical abuse. As also noted earlier, I suspect that both of my parents had just such genetic predispositions.

Experimental animals are bred for a wide range of biomedical research to understand the mechanisms of diseases and to develop therapeutic interventions. We give rodents various forms of cancers for this purpose. There is a very large literature on inducing chronic pain in rodents with peripheral nerve ligation (tying a nerve with surgical thread) and inflammation produced by injecting noxious compounds under the skin with the goal of curing chronic pain and its associated psychological effects. The Human Immunodeficiency Virus that causes AIDS was studied in a monkey model and treatments developed before introducing them into the human population. No investigator enjoys administering such interventions and it is strictly overseen by university veterinary staff, but the work is extremely important.

I was part of a research group in North Carolina that imaged the brain of a woman in her early 20s who was raped between ages 4-7 and was suffering with irritable bowel syndrome and severe abdominal pain after she married an abusive husband. To this point in my life at about age 50 I thought my primary focus should be on pain processing in the brain but this case showed me that in fact my focus should be on harsh physical abuse. It was not only the pain of being raped and abused that she suffered but also the stress associated with such maltreatment. Thus, I spent the next 12 years developing a human-relevant model of harsh physical abuse with the goal to understand what chemical changes occur in their brains; abused children do not surrender their brains for research for obvious reasons. These changes cannot be studied with human imaging methods that have a thick cranium to contend with that is one reason for their lower resolution of brain chemistry. The goal of animal research is to determine how such changes might be understood and reversed or blocked early in adolescence to prevent the ravages of adult onset psychiatric and somatic diseases.

We simulated child abuse with adolescent rabbits using noxious colorectal distension (nCRD). The International Association for the Study of Pain Taxonomy states, "pain is that experience we associate with actual or potential tissue damage. It is unquestionably a sensation in a part of the body, but it is always unpleasant and therefore an emotional experience." By definition, nCRD is potentially tissue damaging and causes unpleasant emotional experience observed in our animals as they squirm, contract their abdominal and other muscles to excrete the balloon and show signs of anxiety when being removed from their cages and during contextual fear testing. This protocol simulates repeated, forced (balloon distender held in place), colorectal stimulation encountered by adolescents in the military, prison, church and families and provides a rare opportunity to study the brain chemical changes evoked by child and adolescent physical abuse and potential therapeutic interventions.

There are, however, things we cannot do with animals such as model human rape itself. This is because animals, as far as we know, do not experience shame, guilt and other forms of higher-order emotional responses associated with rape. We assume for now that they are responding to the pain and stress of their experiences and can test this by analyzing their level of anxiety by demonstrating whether or not they approach the context where they received nCRD. Indeed, some animals do not approach it and are classified as vulnerable, while others do and are resilient. We can evaluate the brain mechanisms of this important dichotomy with high resolution brain sections.

Thus, animal research is providing a window on features of human physical abuse that is not available in human research. Finally, I wrote a commentary for the first volume and issue of *Medical Research Innovation* because the research community does not appear to fully appreciate the model's significance and how to develop such an animal model. Since this is an open access journal, it is available free of charge and I present parts of it here (without references; see online article for them) so the reader, if so inclined, can consider some of the difficulties encountered in attempting to support such research.

Reverse Translation of Child Abuse to an Animal Model

Introduction

Child abuse is a serious problem in American society. With every passing month there are new revelations including that by priests, college coaches, politicians, and sex traffickers. These experiences often leave permanent scars on the brains of the survivors of such abuse that last long into adulthood, are poorly treated and cannot be simply overlooked. Due to the shame associated with it, survivors are less likely to seek what little help there is. Indeed, effective treatment can only emerge from detailed brain studies of what occurs during and after abusive events. One such approach is the use of animal models but this has been impeded by a general misunderstanding by the experimental scientific community of what can and cannot be accomplished with such models. Clarifying these misconceptions is the purpose of the present commentary.

It is important to draw a red line where socially inappropriate behaviors such as groping, sexual harassment and other unwanted advances end and where harsh physical abuse, which we are trying to model, begins. Two reviewers of this work asked, "Were social stimuli considered, i.e., social trauma?" and "Can you really appeal to 'socioeconomic factors' in discussing your results." An animal model cannot address these issues and they are not raised as relevant. Nociceptive (pain)-evoked stress during predatory or disciplinary assault is at issue; not socioeconomics. Severe physical abuse in humans is defined by being hit with an object, burning, or forced penetrative sex at least once a month for at least a year (1 Bremner et al., 1999). The New York City Alliance Against Sexual Assault (web site) states, "adolescents are more likely to experience sexually violent crimes than any other age ... Rape of males is any sexual assault involving forced penetration of the anus or mouth by a penis or other object." Sexual abuse is forced sex and only life-threatening force predicts adult health status (2 3 Leserman et al., 1996, 1997), while abuser gender does not predict symptomatology (4 Briere and Elliot, 2003). Thus, this model we developed emphasizes the early stages of the physical parameters of abuse rather than socioeconomic factors. As discussed below, animal models do not seek a complete replication of the human experience and this may be a virtue.

Human Imaging

Some structural and functional imaging studies report intriguing brain alterations associated with a history of child abuse including but not limited to the anterior cingulate and midcingulate cortices (ACC, MCC; 23 Ringel et al., 2008; 24 Thomaes et al., 2010; 25 Van Harmelen et al., 2010). It is surprising, therefore, that no efforts have been made to reverse translate key issues into an experimental animal model. This translational deficiency means that molecular, cellular and detailed circuit changes evoked by abuse cannot be analyzed and, in the long-term, rational therapeutics cannot be developed proximal to the abusive events to block adult-onset psychopathology. Moreover, a neurobiology of abuse cannot evolve until such a model is available for neuroscientific research. We attribute this failure by the scientific community to a misunderstanding of what child harsh physical abuse is and how to begin the modelling process by first emphasizing the early painful/stressful events; more dynamics such as social interactions can be added to the model as observations accumulate.

Animal Models: General Issues

There are difficulties simulating the human condition in experimental animals, but in many instances the drawbacks in humans can become virtues in animal research. One impediment is heterogeneity; i.e., all children/adolescents have different genetic makeups, find themselves in different contexts during the abuse, the abuse can occur at different times of their life, the relationship of the abuse to evoked symptoms (fear, anxiety, stress, pain) can be quite complex and may evolve over time into different disease states some of which are termed functional pain syndromes like fibromyalgia and some types of temporomandibular joint disorder. Indeed, children do not become aware of their abuse often for decades after the experiences and their reports may only become useful in late adolescence (ages 20-25 and beyond). Thus, there are so many unknowns when working with abused children, it is almost impossible to determine cause and effect in terms of their experiences and brain changes much less devise treatments. We have argued that some of these problems can be overcome with animals and in some instances completely avoided. Failure to develop an animal model may be attributed to this lack of understanding of key abuse issues by the experimental community. Commentaries on research proposals and article submissions on our first work (26 Vogt et al., 2018) provide a sampling of such concerns as noted throughout this commentary.

This brings us to the general issue of using animal models. Of course, all mammals can be abused; however, no neuroscientist thinks that an animal experiences the same perceptions of abuse as humans. Animals are required for 4 reasons. First, the same strain can be used such that genetic differences play a minor role in variability of responses to abuse. Second, the onset, duration, and characteristics of the abuse can be standardized, while in humans these factors can only be estimated, if they are determined at all. Third, although animals cannot tell us about their internal feelings, they can be tested behaviorally and provide a window into their world of abuse. Fourth, the brains can be removed in order to explore protein changes that occur during and after the abusive events. This is a critical issue as it will lead eventually to identifying what networks (connected nodes) are involved and how to fix them soon after the abusive events.

No animal model is an exact replication of any human disorder but rather is used to study aspects of a disease. For example, mice overexpressing amyloid-β peptide and showing memory deficits are a model of Alzheimer's Disease that allows one to assess the synthesis and degradation of this peptide and potential relationships with neurodegeneration and altered behavior; yet no one would claim that this is an exact equivalent to the human disease. This does not negate the model and can be viewed as a strength as some confounding variables in humans are avoided as is the case with our abuse model. For example, although adolescent harsh abuse is influenced by socioeconomic factors (9 Imbierowicz and Egle, 2003), abuse is initiated with intense physical pain and stress, usually by a male predator on a young female, and it is not known what occurs in the brain independent of socioeconomic factors. The physical parameters of the primary abuse event can be simulated experimentally with controlled frequency, duration and amplitude of noxious/stressful stimuli, assessment of single neuron responses and postmortem brains and would show the effects of harsh physical abuse without confounding human psychosocioeconomic factors.

Animals provide a standardized approach to abuse, brain

changes and possible interventions in order to block adult-onset psychopathology. It does not engage socioeconomic factors. The goal of such work is to devise effective treatment strategies that have not emerged from human studies.

An Animal Model of Harsh Adolescent Abuse

The first attempt to model child/adolescent abuse was published by Vogt et al. (26 2018). The abuse was short (21 min) bouts of forced, noxious distension of colorectal tissue (nCRD), 3X/week for 3 weeks. Some neuroscientists have incorrectly assumed this is a form of chronic visceral pain but this is not the case as addressed in the Discussion of this article. In fact, it is a nociceptive-stress model; i.e., pain-evoked stress. The behavioral task of contextual fear showed that some animals were vulnerable to the abuse and others were not (resilient). The study focused mainly on ACC for reasons discussed in the Introduction of this article where there is also a brief consideration of the little we know about the brain imaging in human abused and raped children. Finally, a large portion of this article reports neuronal responses to noxious stimulation and was not written for the layperson; however, the general reader will be engaged by the Introduction, first part of the Methods that describes the model, first part of the Results that describe behavioral results and the Discussion.

Comments on the Abuse Model that Impair Scientific Progress

Reviewers of grant applications and articles for publication provide interesting insights into why a neurobiology of child abuse has not yet gone mainstream. A few quotes from our experience are enlightening beyond those already mentioned above. First, reviewers have the impression that face validity requires all features of human abuse be addressed and this is not the case. One said, "Child physical and sexual abuse can never be accurately modeled in animals. Only cautious parallels can be drawn. The Principle Investigator has laid out too many similarities between humans and the present model." This reviewer is over interpreting what has been done and claimed. It seems that one would seek as many similarities as possible to achieve face validity. Another said, "The validity of nCRD as an ecologically relevant model of adolescent human physical abuse or sexual assault is highly questionable and thus its translational relevance to mechanisms of development of psychopathology ... is also questioned" and another said, "It is hard to understand how this is "a simulation of physical parameters of child abuse." Our article on this subject summarizes the model of the physical parameters of child abuse that includes 1) an age approximating late childhood/early adolescence, 2) painful stimulation (nCRD, 60 mmHg pressure) with the distender simulating the male penis during anal intercourse, 3) short duration stimuli of ~21 min to simulate time to male ejaculation, 4) forced stimulation by holding the distender in place, and 5) repeated events (3X/week for 3 weeks). Thus, the protocol engages conscious pain/stress systems for only a total of ~two hours.

Another issue that is of interest to reviewers is what to call the model. One said, "it is a model of the role of ACC in anticipation, discomfort, pain and anxiety." This is a summary of the functions of ACC and not a correct designation of the model. Another said, "simply define the colorectal distention model alone which is clearly aversive." Yes, it is and must be aversive, but nCRD is only part of the protocol to generate the early stages of human abusive events. Another said, "The paradigm seems more like a model of visceral pain and social isolation and lacks the intra-species, social dyadic components of human abuse or sexual assault." There are many reasons why the model is not one of chronic visceral pain as enumerated in the Discussion by Vogt et al. (26 2018). Further, the animals were not socially isolated and the model does not consider maternal neglect, although a separate study of this issue is justified. The "social dyadic components" have been addressed above. Another statement reads, "Is 'more precise coding of visceral stimuli' a result of reflex visceral motor activity, transduction, inputs of non-visceral with visceral inputs, transmission or processing. How would you know?" We would know this by recording from peripheral and brainstem nuclei engaged in visceral processing such as the nucleus of the Solitary tract. This experiment seems to present a low probability of success as these nuclei are not engaged in the same functions as ACC/MCC as also noted below.

Finally, "The statement that 'such a model would show the effects of harsh physical abuse without confounding human psycho-socio-economic factors' gets at the central problem. The model is repetitive noxious stimuli and many of the effects ... could simply be due to neuroplastic changes at any level of the neuraxis (spinal, thalamic, somatosensory etc.) without having to require any kind of a fear-related or other top-down component." The spinal cord, thalamus and somatosensory cortex are not engaged in contextual fear as tested in this model but the reviewer appears unaware of this literature. Also, there may be many other non-ACC areas in the brain that contribute to child abuse disorder, but different methods will need to be employed to identify them. More importantly, if the reviewer is claiming that fear is not a serious component of repetitive, forced child abuse, he/she is mistaken. A case report by Terr (27 1991) makes this very clear; "A girl was sexually misused by her father from ages 5-15, at which time she ran away ... As a married adult of 38, she feared sex with her husband unless she initiated the act herself. She responded to the female-on-top or side-to-side positions, positions that had not been originally taken by her father. Any sexual positioning that was evocative of the incestuous set of sexual postures stimulated fear, pain, and revulsion." They also ask, "Does this article really have direct implications for sexual function (and) emotional development...?" It appears to be so and, unfortunately, scientific claims and concerns are primarily tangential to the model and its outcomes.

Conclusions

Clearly child abuse is a serious and ongoing problem in our society and has many adult repercussions. Yet, without an animal model, we will never be able to characterize brain plasticities evoked by harsh physical child abuse, with or without aspects of social support, much less develop rational drug therapies for survivors proximal to their abuse. This commentary argues against the key impediments broached by investigators to scientific progress toward these goals. The hope is that these impediments can be overcome to provide hope for survivors through brain research.

Overall Conclusions

IT IS A difficult task laying out for all to read the details of one's life; particularly mine. Indeed, there were times when I became somewhat depressed reliving the details of my strange life. Here we review some of the larger themes considered throughout this investigational psycho-autobiography based on my Lifeline and some general issues relating to larger populations with similar impairments.

I lived with ADHD my entire life and it was the starting point of my harsh physical, parental abuse. Also as many as 20-30% of our society are so afflicted with this adolescent developmental disorder. While ADHD itself is not a form of abuse, it is surprisingly related to adolescent maltreatment and it evokes profound effects on brain organization and functions. The symptoms interfere with most aspects of one's life; cognitive, emotional and social/family relationships. Even driving during late adolescence is significantly impaired and needs close parental guidance. However, the view promulgated in this volume is that the ADHD genes have survival value even in today's society and that as one ages ADHD symptoms can be ameliorated towards social and professional advantage. While even as adults there are ADHD-derived difficulties, do not give in to them but rather use them to your and society's advantage by crossing new boundaries and forcing society to conform to your positive rules rather than in the opposite direction.

Abuse comes in three major forms (physical/sexual, neglect,

emotional). It is my view that frequent abuse is not a stable entity in the brain and different forms can contribute to a cascade of events leading to PTSD, bipolar (BD), borderline personality (BPD) and anxiety disorders, a lack of empathy and enhanced suffering. This is certainly my experience. While a survivor may have been raised under one form of abuse, breaking the Cycle of Violence requires understanding all forms of abuse to avoid perpetuating abuse in and outside of one's family. This is a point at which I failed, although not in a way that I predicted. Although I did not physically abuse or neglect my children, there was emotional abuse that I did not understand until this last decade. Identifying the form of one's abuse aids in seeking psychotherapeutic and drug treatments as well as raising a family.

While artistic expression provides an outlet for survivors and can play a role in transitioning to a new life as it did for me, it should be supplemented with psychotherapy, possibly meditation, biofeedback, relaxation and other forms of healthy conduct that helps to relieve stress. Abuse of alcohol, cocaine and other life-threatening substances will only perpetuate the abuse memories and further damage the brain, liver, heart and other organs. Drugs that ameliorate stress, anxiety and depression, however, should be considered in combination with various forms of psychotherapy such as Dialectical Behavioral Therapy (DBT) and these are discussed in the context of my psychopathologies. While Ritalin and Vyvance are often given to adolescents with ADHD, Ritalin additionally improves the outcomes of DBT for patients with comorbid ADHD and BPD.

An important proviso when considering my brain damage and trying to relate it to my aberrant behaviors and generalizing to the readers experiences is the fact that I suffered with ADHD, abuse, BD, BPD and PTSD. Vignette 3 shows an image in which many of these pathologies were merged and suggests that at least a summation of brain damage may evoke changes in aMCC beyond those reported as symptoms for each separate syndrome. I conclude that the resulting damage may not be stable and evolves over time as shown in the second figure in Vignette 1. Thus, for example, an individual with only ADHD may not experience the disordered behavioral changes that I report in this psychoautobiography. The additional core deficits I report (breaking boundaries and significantly reduced fear of threats) may be a result of this combined damage, although I suspect they are significantly related to ADHD.

Men and women often have different priorities that can cause friction in the family and this friction can lead to emotional abuse of children. Women tend to prioritize family first and career second, while males take the opposite approach including a high emphasis on financial issues. When one considers the additional layer of abuse in either spouse, it likely will add to conflict. In my early fragmented birth family, for example, I did not have a clear understanding of what a healthy family was and how it operated including strong bonds and support among its members. Due to my early neglect, I lacked empathy for others; in other words, my staying mentally above water was my main concern as there was little or no concern for others in my birth family. I attribute my lack of empathy to the many psychopathologies that impaired my MCC and other brain areas. The more brain damage one suffers, it can lead to significant shutting down of normal brain functions. Apparently it is difficult for survivors to clear the demons from their past and the issues that were tender throughout my birth family life still are today to some extent. My wife argues, as any healthy normal would, that people change. This is true to some extent as demonstrated by me and my daughter with DBT. However, at 72 I am not yet nor will I ever be allowed to live with the brain I have with genetic mutations and abuse damage that evolved into other forms of psychiatric disease (PTSD) and further brain damage.

During my adolescence I engaged in relaxation therapy in the woods, basement and a trip to Canada, however, these were accidental forms of relieving stress rather than guided by any rigorous psychiatric technique. During my Transitional Period, I engaged in some artistic efforts to express my internal suffering, although I was also unaware of this as a therapeutic approach. During that time I took the route to dealing with my abuse-damaged brain to work toward understanding and curing chronic pain that is evoked by adolescent abuse. Unfortunately, the truly innovative science that is required for analyzing and treating the abused brain is not understood or financially supported.

I was part of the Cycle of Violence that began with Stanley in the Bronx. His physical abuse of me and Blanche's physical abuse, neglect and emotional abuse combined to enhance the difficulties of an adolescent dealing with ADHD; although this disorder was unknown at the time. I too was aggressive and violent in many ways fulfilling this theory's predictions. It appears that understanding one's abuse can help break the Cycle of Violence and avoid perpetuating it in future generations thus reducing the overall violence in one's family and society in general.

While it is possible to read this book and overlook the cingulate neuroscience/neuropathology; that would be a disservice to your in-depth understanding of what ADHD and abuse survivors are struggling with. Such perspectives raise new questions and confirm whether or not therapeutic approaches have organic brain efficacy. This summary so far has not fully integrated the neuroscience perspective. Stating that critical parts of the brain shrink and have impaired connectivity provides a sense of the task we are up against and it is not trivial, but let us consider a few specific examples of neuroscience insights.

The role of genetic variations in ADHD that are familial is associated with shrinkage in emotional and to a lesser extent cognitive parts of the limbic system. Once this reorganization occurs it may not be reversible but can be ameliorated with Ritalin and Vyvance and DBT. For example, it may be that while neurons shrink and become less functional, they can swell back to their normal size and/or their dendrites may proliferate.

Repetitive abuse likely accumulates damage in our limbic systems and that is the reason reporters of abuse are so important. It must be stopped as soon as possible to limit brain damage.

I am certain that many parents do not understand the consequences of neglectful and emotional abuse, much less what they are. Also, Americans are too willing to use corporal punishment that evokes aggression in their children due to dysregulation of our limbic motor systems. They do not understand that they are conditioning their children to respond in a negative way to themselves and their environment; i.e., the context of their abuse that will last in their brains for their lives.

Maltreatment and PTSD impact anterior cingulate and midcingulate cortices (ACC and MCC, respectively) and this is why they are so often comorbid. While we can localize the sites of brain damage, it cannot be reversed and drug therapies are helpful but do not resolve their brain damage. DBT has been shown to resurrect the thickness of ACC and to some extent MCC and suggests that we are on the path to viable therapies. However, shrinkage and thickening of parts of the limbic system still are not understood in terms of what exactly is changing in the brain; neurons, dendrites, and/or axons? My suggestions above are purely speculation on these mechanisms.

Experienced individuals at mindfulness of breathing show improvement in pACC function that is not observed in non-meditators. In fact, stress and pain relief is rather associated with changes in MCC. It is a striking fact that these procedures may successively alter functions in different parts of cingulate cortex. Although not studied in abuse survivors, this technique may be modified to reduce impairments in such patients. While the basic science is still lacking, such an approach should be considered.

Drugs seek out their receptors in the brain and this provides a viable approach to treating some abuse survivors. In conjunction with psychotherapy this can be a powerful approach as some drugs enhance activity in ACC that mediates emotion.

It appears that extensive damage to MCC greatly reduces empathy for others and is likely a substrate of sociopathic and psychopathic behaviors as well as those in abuse survivors. Improving empathy through rigorous psychotherapy appears necessary to overcome this problem and could be associated with enhancing MCC function over time.

Suffering is associated with functional changes in the limbic system.

Overall Conclusions

While psychotherapists are aware of these problems, the family and companions of abuse survivors need to engage in helping to alleviate them as it often leads to abuse of non-prescription drugs for self-medication. These drugs seek out mainly ACC and MCC and provide survivors with resolution but often lead to abuse liability associated with other parts of the limbic system not discussed herein.

The Cycle of Violence is an environmental series of events that we do not understand from a neurological perspective. How is it transferred from one generation to the next? Is it a series of automatic learning events? How do brain changes occur that lead to such devastating aggression and violence?

The Dalai Lama. I have frequently considered whether or not I should share my views of organized, fundamentalist religions as they are so negative and could offend many readers. I decided to stick with the facts and views that were generated in me by my parents and at bible college. Although I am an atheist, this does not mean I am free of morals, compassion and love for those who suffer like me and in other ways. I long ago decided my views are more closely aligned with those of Buddhists and indeed they are. In 1998 I met the Dalai Lama and his retinue at a small scientific meeting in Arizona. He is the political and spiritual leader of the Chinese province of Tibet and a few of his quotes are notable in relation to what you have read in this volume. "Love is the absence of judgement." Marco was an amazingly loving (non-judgmental) man in how he handled my issues. "People take different roads seeking fulfillment and happiness. Just because they're not on your road doesn't mean they've gotten lost." While I have expressed very significant and negative views of strict, fundamentalist religions, this should not be interpreted that all are on the wrong path to happiness and resolution of pain and suffering. Finally, "A disciplined mind leads to happiness, and an undisciplined mind leads to suffering." Even the trip to Canada produced a disciplined mind that in itself was helpful in reducing my suffering.

I have shared my life, pain, suffering and insights for survivors, their families and companions in the hope that they will achieve happiness and success much sooner than in their 70s. Two issues must be considered. First, putting aside shame, embarrassment and fear, one needs to engage in a frontal assault on the specific problems we survivors face with someone like Marco and/or a companion; face-to-face, excited, committed to moving forward and with great love and compassion. Second, a willingness to take any steps necessary toward resolution of these problems. Many approaches have been suggested in the previous pages in the hope you will consider all your options and not be locked into just one perspective. You do not want to find yourself writing a book at 72 years of age that finally leads to an understanding of what your life has meant. This is a sad outcome of my lifelong struggle. Take these steps at 20 or 30 if you can, so the remainder of your life will be spent in peace with yourself, family and others.

Good luck finding yourself and those around you.

www.ingramcontent.com/pod-product-compliance
Lightning Source LLC
Chambersburg PA
CBHW061252230426
43665CB00026B/2917